Reading Strategies for University Students

Kathleen Romstedt ▪ Julia Tevis McGory

The American Language Program
Ohio State University

Reading Strategies for University Students

COLLIER
MACMILLAN

Library of Congress Cataloging-in-Publication Data

Romstedt, Kathleen.
　　Reading strategies for university students / Kathleen Romstedt,
　Julia Tevis McGory.
　　　　p.　　cm.
　　ISBN 0-02-403430-4
　　1. Reading (Higher education)　2. English language—Study and
　teaching (Higher)　3. College readers.　I. McGory, Julia Tevis.
　II. Title.
　LB2395.3.R66 1988　　　　　　　　　　　　　　87-30868
　428.4′07′11—dc19　　　　　　　　　　　　　　　CIP

Collier Macmillan Canada, Inc.

Coverphoto: Jil P. Robbins
"Out to Lunch" is a lifesized bronze sculpture by American artist J.
Seward Johnson, Jr. Reproduction by permit of Sculpture Placement,
LTD of Washington, D.C.

Printing:　1 2 3 4 5 6 7　　　Year:　8 9 0 1 2 3 4

Collier Macmillan
866 Third Avenue
New York, NY 10022

Printed in the U.S.A.

ISBN 0-02-403430-4

Introduction

Reading Strategies for University Students is written for high intermediate to advanced non-native speakers of English for academic purposes and native speakers at the secondary or university level who need to develop their academic reading skills. The purpose of this text is to provide these students with practice in reading and understanding full-length, unsimplified materials representative of those read in university classes and to help them develop the reading strategies necessary for success in universities where English is the medium of instruction.

Students learn to read by reading. Successful reading is an active process whereby the adult reader brings previously acquired knowledge and experience to the act of reading. The selections in this text are of a general academic nature with exercises designed to facilitate comprehension by drawing on this knowledge and experience. A variety of exercises focus on the strategies essential to comprehension, such as making inferences, examining context for clues to unfamiliar vocabulary, and recognizing organizational devices used within the readings. Successful reading also requires motivation on the part of the reader. Selections must be interesting and relevant. To this end, we have chosen themes relevant to their needs as university students. These themes include business, social science, humanities, biological science, and agriculture.

Each chapter includes a central reading and a shorter related reading. These readings generally are taken from two sources: undergraduate university textbooks and general interest periodicals for adult readers such as *Scientific American, Omni,* and *Psychology Today*.

For each central reading, exercises have been developed that focus on the skills necessary for comprehension. Because the exercises have been written to complement a particular reading, rather than to adhere to a specific format, they include all or some of the following, depending on the nature of the reading.

1. The **Discussion** activates students' knowledge of the content and stimulates interest.
2. The **Preview** of the selection is designed to preview content and organization.
3. The **True or False** section checks comprehension of information directly from the text.
4. The **Reading Worksheet** takes the reader chronologically through the selection and focuses on any number of difficulties as they arise.

It encourages the students to view the selection as a whole rather than in fragmented parts.

5. The **Inference and Restatement** exercise allows students to use their own knowledge in conjunction with the text in order to more fully comprehend the selection.

6. The **Outlining/Skills Checkup** exercises help the students to identify the main ideas of the reading and their organization. These provide the basis for successful note-taking strategies.

7. The **Vocabulary from Context** exercise is designed to familiarize the students with the thought processes involved in grasping the meaning of unfamiliar vocabulary.

8. The **Summary** exercise requires the students to demonstrate their recognition and understanding of the main ideas of the reading as well as their familiarity with key vocabulary items.

9. The **Essay Questions** act as a culminating exercise in which the students are asked to digest what they have read and respond to questions that require support from the reading.

The related reading in each chapter is presented in one of two ways: (1) as a preview reading to introduce the concepts, or (2) as a follow-up intended to give a new perspective to the ideas found in the central selection.

We believe that when given the opportunity to tackle real academic readings and the skills necessary to do it, students can develop the reading strategies necessary for successful university study. It is our hope that *Reading Strategies for University Students* affords them this opportunity.

Acknowledgments

We wish to express our appreciation to our colleagues and our reviewers for their valuable suggestions as we prepared our manuscript. We would also like to thank our husbands, Karl and John, for their active support of this endeavor.

K.R.
J.T.M.

Contents

Reading Strategies for University Students

Social
Interaction

1

Prereading

DISCUSSION

Directions: Read the following questions. Be prepared to discuss them.

1. How do you think we learn our native languages? Who teaches us? Does anyone teach us?

2. Is it possible for a person who cannot hear to learn to speak?

3. What do you think learning a language involves?

4. What were some of the first words you said?

5. What do you think the following phrase means: "Actions speak louder than words"?

PREVIEW

Directions: Read the title and any subheadings of the selection. Also look at the illustrations and read any captions. Then, without reading the chapter, answer the following questions.

1. This selection is from a chapter in a psychology textbook. Look at the title of the first section, "Acquisition and Use of Language." What do you think is the relationship between language and psychology?

   _____

   _____

2. How many main sections are there in the chapter? Where did you find this information?

   _____

3. Look at the subheadings within the selection. There are three sections. What are they?

   a. _____

    b. _____

    c. _____

4. What three processes are involved in language learning?

    a. _____

    b. _____

    c. _____

5. How many stages of language development are there? _____

6. Look at Figure 1–3. Look at the symbols in the illustration. What happens to the representation of the idea as it moves from speaker to listener?

_____

_____

READING

SOCIAL INTERACTION

1   Upon returning to college in the fall, a student reported: "This past summer I taught reading at an elementary school in a low-income area of Philadelphia. The students' ages ranged from 6 to 13, and with the older students discipline was a major problem. Fights always seemed to spring up out of name-calling and baiting. During the arguments, the uninvolved kids remained silent, but sometimes they gathered in small clusters with their friends. However, as soon as the fists began to fly, crowds of kids surrounded the fighters. The staff of the program experimented with several techniques to discipline the fights, but by far the most successful was to remove the fighters to another room, away from the other kids, shut the door, and tell them to go ahead and fight. Then the fight ended. Are physical fights promoted by an audience of observers?"

2   The question raised by this student concerns the influence of a social setting on behavior, which is the basic topic of this chapter. This issue has been considered briefly at several previous points in this book, but here we encounter it directly. Simply defined, this whole field, called _social psychology,_ is the study of our responsiveness to one another.

Acquisition and Use of Language

3   One of the most obvious ways in which we respond to one another is through language. Without language, there would be far less social behavior among human beings. In a sense, language is *the* fabric of our society.

Processes in Language Learning

4   Because of the complexity of human language and its vital role in society, the acquisition of language has been called the most significant achievement in a person's life. In fact, one psychologist has said: "The development of langauge in an individual is the growth of the human mind in that person." But how do children learn language? For example, how did the children in the Philadelphia school learn to engage in name-calling, baiting, and more normal discourse?

5   **Role of Modeling.** The casual observer probably would say that imitation, or *modeling*, is the crucial factor. The child copies some model, such as a parent or other adult, according to social learning theory. Thus, one child learns Portuguese and another learns English. Within the English-speaking world, one child acquires an Australian accent and another learns to speak like a Texan. The use of idioms also is acquired through modeling. The Irish child says "half ten," while the American child says "ten-thirty." Examples in support of modeling are endless. Clearly the child learns what sounds to make, when to make them, and how to put them together partly by this process. But there is more involved.

6   If children learn only by mimicking, how do we account for their predictable errors not found in adult language? For example, a little girl says "What means it?" when she wants to know the meaning of a word. Her parents say "What does it mean?" Similarly, the child says "hisself," while the parents say "himself." Further, how do we explain the fact that deaf children learn to speak? Helen Keller lost her capacity for vision and hearing at age 18 months, yet she mastered the use of English not as a series of mechanical signals but as an instrument of thought (Figure 1–1).

7   **Conditioning Processes.** In addition to modeling, when one is learning vocabulary and tonal expressions, the *conditioning processes* also seem important. The child learns to attach certain meanings to certain symbols, and often the relationship is arbitrary. The little girl learns the word "book" in connection with this thing you are now reading, but it might have been called "desk," "cloud," "bag," or anything else, as far as the child is concerned. In the classical conditioning tradition, the learning process takes place as the word "book" is spoken or written on several occasions when the object is present. After many such associations, the child recognizes the word as a substitute for the thing.

8   Operant conditioning also occurs. For example, the child says "book" and receives some sort of reinforcement; she is given a book, or a parent reads to her. As a result, the child uses words more and more. In terms of two-factor theory, it appears that word meanings are acquired essentially through classical conditioning

FIGURE 1–1. Helen Keller's Ability. *The reasoning process is especially important in true language acquisition, as demonstrated by the blind-deaf Helen Keller, who suddenly discovered in a flash that everything can have a name. One morning during her seventh year, Helen patted the hand of Miss Sullivan, her teacher, and pointed to running water, signifying that she wanted to know its name. At this time, Helen knew a few words, but only in a rote manner; she did not know how to use the words or that everything could be named.*

The word "water" was spelled out on her hand in the manual alphabet and later, while she was filling a cup at the pump, it was spelled for her again. This time the cold water was overflowing on her free hand, and the spelling of the word at the same time had a remarkable effect, which Miss Sullivan describes in the following way:

"The word, coming so close upon the sensation of cold water rushing over her hand seemed to startle her. She dropped the mug and stood as one transfixed. A new light came into her face. She spelled water several times. Then she dropped to the ground and asked for its name and pointed to the pump and the trellis, and suddenly turning round she asked for my name. I spelled 'Teacher.' Just then the nurse brought Helen's little sister into the pump-house and Helen spelled 'baby' and pointed to the nurse. All the way back to the house she was highly excited, and learned the name of every object she touched, so that in a few hours she had added 30 new words to her vocabulary." (Library of Congress)

and word usage is acquired through the operant process.

9   **Information Processing.** However, the conditioning processes, in turn, appear inadequate as an explanation of language learning when the child begins combining words and intonations in a systematic way. Then they become sentences, not random words, and permit the enormous variety of nuances of meaning that are characteristic of a true language. Children often make correct grammatical constructions even though they have never previously heard the particular sequence of sounds. At some level, the child is formulating and following "rules" about how the language works. Even the child's incorrect grammatical constructions, such as "teached" and "hitted," suggest that the speaker is following some rule.

10   In recent years, studies of language acquisition in older children have moved away from the conditioning approach towards the more creative aspects of language postulated in the *information processing* approach, focusing particularly upon the structure of language. In this approach, the process of reasoning by analogy, in which the child knows "wait-waited" and therefore says "teach-teached," has received a great deal of attention. When these overgeneralizations occur regularly, children show that they are acquiring the rules of grammar. On such bases, langauge is regarded as a creative activity on the part of the child, based in hereditary capacities, not a "stamping in" process on the part of the environment.

11   In summary, all three processes seem to be involved—modeling, conditioning, and information processing—and all of these modes of learning have been examined in detail in previous chapters. To paraphrase an earlier comment, a more complete understanding of the interrelationships among these processes in the acquisition of language will constitute, in many respects, a more complete understanding of the operation of the human mind.

Stages of Language Development

12   Like the other aspects of human development, the acquisition of language can be roughly characterized in terms of stages. Certain predictable changes occur in every normal child as he or she matures. While the rate of these changes varies from child to child, the sequence of stages is essentially the same for all normal children.

13   **Cooing.** The first vocalizations of human infants are unpatterned sounds. They consist of crying, gurgling, a few other noises, and *cooing*, particuarly when the infant is contented. During this early period, the infant's speech mechanisms continue to mature, perhaps partly as a result of this vocal activity. Some of these sounds also have reward value, bringing a parent or other caretaker to tend the infant's needs.

14   The infant hears the cooing that he or she makes and, through muscular involvement, probably senses the motor aspects as well. This auditory and kinesthetic feedback may be further reinforcing, as a form of self-stimulation.

15   **Babbling.** Gradually, there is a transition from cooing to *babbling*, in which a particular sound pattern is repeated consistently, as in "da-da-da" and "lal-lal-lal-lal." This behavior becomes prevalent about the fifth month and clearly represents greater

control over the speech mechanisms than the earlier unpatterned cooing. In babbling, the baby's noises include many of the important sounds found in adult speech and, in fact, these babbling sounds are similar in all normal babies. Research has demonstrated that European, American, Asiatic, and other babies cannot be distinguished from one another on the basis of the vocalizations at this stage.

16 **Word Recognition.** Around the eighth to eleventh month, the typical baby begins to distinguish the meaningful sounds in the language that he or she hears. Since these sounds almost always appear in words, this stage is known as *word recognition*, and it consistently appears before word usage. The baby gradually begins to show an understanding of intonations, words, and phrases, although of course this learning continues for several years.

17 A way to test an infant's word recognition is to observe the baby's response in a given situation. Late in the first year, for example, the infant clearly learns to avoid things said to be *hot*, although the child has no special sound to represent hotness.

18 **First Use of Words.** The infant's first word, usually indistinguishable from babbling except by fond parents, is almost invariably a name of some sort. Hence, this next stage is called *naming* or *first words*, and it generally appears around the twelfth month, when a single word sometimes represents a whole phrase or sentence. When something is hot, the infant now gives it a name. Most likely he or she says "ta" because the front consonants, explosives such as *p* and *t*, and nasals such as *m* and *n*, are more readily produced than those from the back of the throat.

However, the back vowels, such as *a* in "mama," are the first to appear. Hence, it is no accident that "mama" and "papa" are such universal names for parents around the globe.

19 **Using Words in Combination.** The beginning of language ability, however, according to many experts, is not the child's first word. It occurs when the child first puts words together. Prior to this event, we cannot speak of an active grammar or language system. The normal human child achieves this developmental landmark of using words in combinations sometime between the first and second year.

20 These first word combinations are known as *telegraphic utterances* because, like telegrams, they are highly abbreviated but contain the most important elements. Thus, the mother says, "Now your toy is lost." The child responds, "Toy lost." The father says, "Let's go to the tennis court." The child replies, "Go tennis." Gradually, these expressions grow longer and longer and become less telegraphic in style. (Figure 1–2).

21 **Complex Constructions.** After learning to combine words, the next problem is *syntax*, which refers to the order in which words, phrases, and clauses are used in a given language. Language almost always requires a certain sequence. There is a very important difference between "Tom hit Sally" and "Sally hit Tom".

22 Children's efforts to master word order are illustrated in *grammatical transformations*, which require changes in word forms and sentence construction with various expressions. Children learn, for example, that in simple statements the subject generally appears before the verb. They also learn that the "wh" words, such as "what," "why," and "when," always

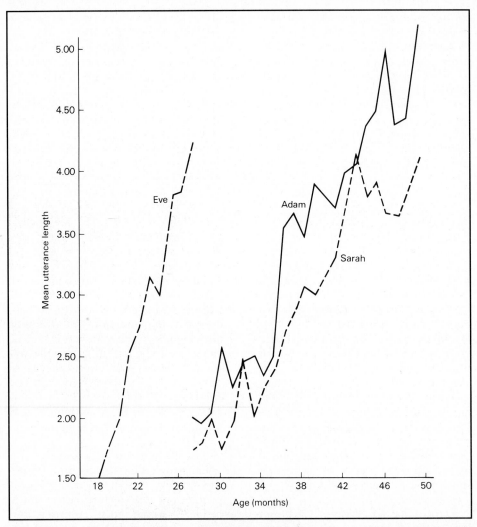

FIGURE 1–2. Combining Words. The graph shows the mean length of utterance in relation to age. Mean length of utterance is defined as the average number of language units with distinct meanings in a given expression. For example, "Daddy chair" would be scored as 2 and "Give me the ball" would be rated as 4. The mean length of utterance rises steadily with age, although a given child may be consistently ahead of or behind others of the same age.

come first in questions. Thus, their first "wh" questions become "Where I should put it?" and "What he can ride in?" Only gradually does the child learn to change the positions of the subject and auxiliary verb in these instances, asking "What can he ride in?" and so forth. Interestingly, when the "wh" word is not involved, the child readily reverses the subject and auxiliary verb to form a question, such as "Can he ride in it?" When first learning to form questions, the child apparently can master one change, the inclusion of the "wh" word *or* the change in sequence, but not both together.

23   By six years of age, the normal child has acquired most of the basic grammatical constructions of his or her language. At this stage, children are highly adept at using language as an expressive tool, as illustrated in the behavior of the Philadelphia children, cited at the beginning of this chapter. Vocabulary development, of course, continues for many years.

A Communication Model

24   The communication between fighters in the Philadelphia schools included name-calling and baiting, as well as blows with the fists. Communication also occurred between the fighters and the audience, which quickly gathered. In simplest terms, *communication* involves the transmission of information from a source to a receiver. It can occur between inanimate objects, as when the thermostat sends a "turn on" signal to the furnace, or between living organisms, as just illustrated.

25   In understanding the communication process, it is sometimes useful to refer to a model containing these major components: an encoder, signals, a channel, and a decoder. The *encoder* sends a message by selecting and transmitting various signals. These *signals* may be words, gestures, dots and dashes, or some other representation. They are any signs or symbols that have meaning, and they are transmitted to someone else via a communication *channel*, such as sound waves or printed pages. The *decoder* receives the signals and interprets them, thus obtaining the message. As you read this page, you decode the letter arrangement, and in the Philadelphia schools, the combatants decoded sounds and gestures. The process is not a simple one, however, because the same signals can have different meanings for different people, and outside influences can distort the communication. (Figure 1–3).

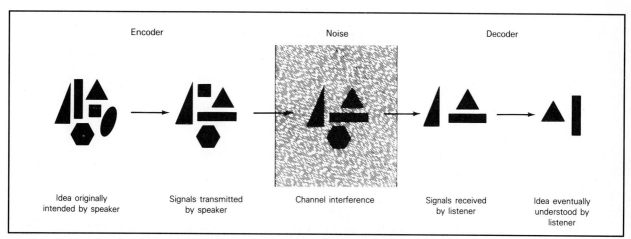

Encoder   Noise   Decoder

Idea originally intended by speaker   Signals transmitted by speaker   Channel interference   Signals received by listener   Idea eventually understood by listener

FIGURE 1–3.   A Communication Model. In communication theory, noise interferes with the transmission of a message. It can involve interfering signals from another communication or interference within the same channel, as in radio transmission static.

26 **Verbal Meanings.** The signals transmitted in the Philadelphia setting were both verbal and nonverbal. A *verbal* signal is one that involves words, and the powerful influence of this form of communication is known to all of us. In many respects, words are the binding force in society, and this form of communication has been considered in many contexts throughout this book. But so far we have focused only on denotative meanings. The *denotative meaning* of a word or other symbol points to tive meanings. Such meanings give the skillful writer or speaker a powerful expressive tool, but at the same time they increase the possibilities for misunderstanding.

28 **Nonverbal Signals.** When the signals do not involve words, they are called *nonverbal*, and this form of communication may seem of small significance until we look at it more closely. Then we discover that it is extremely prevalent, often efficient, and sometimes quite subtle. In

---

■ Recently, a friend of mine died in a tragic accident. His close friends, also close friends of mine, were extremely emotionally upset by this event and I felt I should try to help. But what can one say? I have never known anyone to know the right words to say or how to say them in a situation such as this. Finally, I approached one of my friends, and grasped his hand tightly and held it. Nothing was said, but I think he knew what I meant.

---

something; it denotes something specific and generally does not cause much confusion. The denotative meaning of the word "pencil" is much the same for all of us—an elongated object containing graphite that is used for writing.

27 On the other hand, *connotative meaning* concerns abstract qualities or properties, often with emotional implications. The denotative meaning of the word "pig" is a four-legged mammal with coarse bristles, but when this word is used with reference to a human being, the connotative meaning suggests that this person is unclean, greedy, or obese, since the denotation clearly does not apply. This example gives the merest hint of the nuances that are added to language by connota-

many cases, nonverbal communication can express one's intention more adequately than words, as illustrated in the schoolyard fisticuffs. ■

29 Every society employs several forms of nonverbal communication, including gestures, postures, and various objects. *Gestures* with special communicative significance include facial expression, head-shaking, and hand movements, but these actions may have different meanings in different cultures. For example, an American boy in Madrid was chastised by his Spanish teacher for responding improperly to her hand-waving, which was intended as a beckoning signal. To him, it meant that he should move farther away.

30 One's *posture* constitutes another category of nonverbal signals. A boy

prepared to fight may stand firmly erect, as though he is "master of all he surveys," while his opponent, in utter despair, may withdraw in a stooped manner. Much has been written about "reading" another person's thoughts by decoding his or her different postures, especially in a business conference. These findings are suggestive, but they are not well documented.

31   Less obvious than gestures or postures, but still with communicative significance, are the *objects* that a person possesses, such as books, a baseball bat, and a new suit. A barrier across the road tells us that we should go no farther; the junk lying by the roadside tells us that someone has been careless, if not malicious. The reader need only look around to discover the many subtle and obvious instances of nonverbal communication and to appreciate their significance in human behavior.

32   **Multiple Signals.**   Human communication also involves *multiple signals* in which several verbal and nonverbal messages are sent and received almost simultaneously. A person says "Hello" while smiling and shaking hands; a successful storyteller captures audience interest in many ways.

33   Sometimes these signals contradict one another. A female student tells her professor that she really likes the course, but she often misses class and forgets assignments. A man explained to one of the authors that he was no longer upset by his divorce, yet he had a sad look on his face. The complexities of the communication process have prompted research not only on the meanings of verbal and nonverbal signals but also on the interaction between them.

—From Lloyd Dodge Fernald and Peter S. Fernald, *Basic Psychology*, 4th edition, Chapter 14, William C. Brown Publishers, Iowa, 1979.

Postreading

TRUE OR FALSE

Directions: Decide if each of the following statements is True (T) or False (F) based on the selection.

_____ 1. The predictable errors that children make while learning a language are due to incorrect modeling.

_____ 2. Word meanings and word usages are acquired through conditioning processes.

_____ 3. Helen Keller's story demonstrates that modeling is important to language learning.

_____ 4. Learning a language is complex and involves more than one process.

_____ 5. All children go through the same basic stages of development, although the order of these stages varies from child to child.

_____ 6. Children comprehend words before they produce them.

_____ 7. A child is able to express almost anything in words by the age of six.

_____ 8. Although it would be difficult, communication can occur without a decoder.

_____ 9. The connotative meaning of a word is the same as the concrete meaning.

_____10. When a child says, "Where I should put it?" he or she makes a mistake because his or her understanding of language lacks the knowledge of grammar.

READING WORKSHEET

Directions: After you have completed the true-or-false exercise, answer the following questions. You may refer to the selection if necessary.

1. What is the purpose of paragraphs 1 and 2?

_____

_____

2. In paragraph 2, what does *this issue* refer to?

_____

3. How is social psychology defined?

_____

_____

4. Why is *the* set in italics in paragraph 3?

_____

5. What mental image comes to mind when you read the word *fabric*?

_____

What is the author trying to convey by using this word?

_____

6. The author asks two questions in paragraph 4. What do you expect the author to do next?

_____

_____

Which question serves as a transitional sentence?

_____

_____

7. What does the quotation in paragraph 4 mean?

_____

_____

8. Find the synonym for *modeling* in the first sentence of paragraph 5. Find another in paragraph 6. Why do you think the author uses these synonyms?

_____

_____

9. After reading paragraph 5, choose the best paraphrase of the social learning theory.
   a. Children learn words their parents teach them.
   b. Children learn by imitating adults in society.
   c. Children learn the language of society.

10. What are the two questions asked in paragraph 6 that the modeling theory cannot answer?

    a. _____

    b. _____

11. Give an example of a "predictable error" not found in adult language.

    _____

12. What technique is used throughout the article to indicate important terminology?

    _____

13. Read paragraph 7 carefully. Copy the sentence that explains the classical conditioning process.

    _____

    _____

    Which sentence gives an example of an "arbitrary" relationship?

    _____

    _____

14. What are the parts of the two-factor theory (paragraph 8)?

    a. _____

    b. _____

15. Why would a child say "teached" and "hitted" instead of the correct past tense forms? _____

    _____

16. In paragraph 10, what does *these overgeneralizations* refer to?

    _____

What are overgeneralizations?

_____

_____

17. An earlier statement is paraphrased in paragraph 11. Find this sentence, then locate the original sentence and write it here.

_____

_____

18. Write a paraphrase of the last sentence in paragraph 12.

_____

_____

19. Why might an infant coo?

_____

_____

20. At which stage in development do babies develop sounds specific to their native language? _____

_____

21. Why do children all over the world refer to their parents as "mama" and "papa"? _____

_____

22. Give another example of telegraphic speech (paragraph 20) not given in the text.

a. parent: _____

b. child: _____

23. Look at Figure 1–2. Answer the following questions.

a. Who conducted the study? _____

b. Who were the subjects? _____

    c. What is being compared? _____

    d. What are the results? _____

24. Explain why "Where I can go?" is formed, according to one of the rules in paragraph 22. _____

_____

25. Read the section on the communication model (paragraphs 24 through 27).

    a. What does a communication model represent?

_____

    b. List the parts of the model.

_____

26. Why would it be more difficult to decode connotative meanings as opposed to denotative meanings?

_____

_____

27. What are some connotative meanings that you can suggest for the word *snake* when it is applied to a person?

_____

_____

_____

28. What does the square (■) at the end of paragraph 28 signal?

_____

29. What message is communicated by a coat hanging on the back of an empty chair in the library?

_____

30. Why does the use of multiple signals make the understanding of language complex?

_____

INFERENCE AND RESTATEMENT

Directions: Decide whether each of the following is a restatement (R), an infer-ence (I), or a false statement (F) according to the selection. If the sentence is a restatement, locate the original in the selection and give the paragraph number where it is found.

_____ **1.** A baby indicates contentment by cooing.

_____ **2.** Some forms of nonverbal communication are different from country to country.

_____ **3.** Children learn what to say and how and when to say it partially by imitating adults.

_____ **4.** A child who says "putted" instead of "put" is demonstrating that he or she knows that regular verbs in English end in *-ed*.

_____ **5.** The denotation of a word is more or less exact because it refers to a specific object.

_____ **6.** A person who employs multiple signals in communication can relay more information to the listener than someone who only verbalizes.

_____ **7.** Any given word always means the same thing to all of the speakers of that language.

_____ **8.** Children learn the most common sounds in their parents' lan-guage first.

_____ **9.** Language is one means by which all societies are held together.

_____**10.** Children can learn only one language at a time.

OUTLINING

Directions: Below is a partial outline of "Acquisition and Use of Language" from "Social Interaction." Reread the selection and complete the outline.

I. Acquisition and use of language

    A. Processes in language learning

1. Modeling

    a) Explanation: Modeling occurs when a child learns to speak by imitating other speakers of the same language.

        (1) Example: _____

    b) Problems with the theory

        (1) _____

        (2) _____

2. Conditioning processes

    a) Classical conditioning

        (1) Explanation: The child learns to attach _____

        _____ .

            (a) Example: _____

    b) _____

        (1) Explanation: _____

        _____

            (a) Example: _____

        _____

3. _____

    1. Explanation: _____

        a) Words are formed when _____

        _____ .

            (1) Example: _____

        b) Overgeneralization occurs when _____

        _____ .

            (1) Example: _____

Using this same general pattern, outline the next section, "Stages of Language Development," on another sheet of paper.

Vocabulary from Context

Directions: *Using your own knowledge and information from the text, define the following words. Refer to the selection while you work. Don't be afraid to guess.*

1. capacity (paragraph 6)
    Read the sentence containing this term. Who was Helen Keller?

    Capacity means _____.

2. arbitrary (paragraph 7)
    The third sentence in the paragraph gives you a clue to the meaning of this word.

    Arbitrary means _____.

3. inanimate (paragraph 24)
    In the final sentence, examples of inanimate objects are given, then a contrast (signaled by *or*) is added in the last phrase of the sentence.

    Inanimate means _____.

4. combatants (paragraph 25)
    The story that opens the selection contains a synonym of this word.

    Combatants means _____.

5. nuances (paragraph 27)
    The paragraph gives examples of nuances of the word *pig*.

    Nuances means _____.

Summary

Directions: *Fill in the blanks so that the following summary is logical, grammatically correct, and accurate according to the selection.*

_____ is the principal means through which human beings _____ with one another. Children acquire language in several _____, the first of which is called _____. In this stage, infants make _____ with no particular pattern. _____, which is the _____ stage of language development, consists of

_____ syllables or sound sets such as "ma-ma-ma-ma." The third stage is _____ recognition. It is during this _____ that babies from eight to eleven _____ begin to _____ the meanings which certain sounds or _____ have. The next _____ is referred to as _____ or "first words." In this stage, a _____ begins to produce sounds that clearly intend _____, even though the word may not be understood by all listeners.

Next, a child begins to use words in _____. Two-, three-, and four-word phrases make up _____ utterances in which only the most important _____ appear. In the final stage, a child begins _____ complex _____. By the age of six, _____ children have a strong basic control of the _____ patterns of their own languages.

Successful development of language is part of the _____ upon which _____ with others will be built.

ESSAY QUESTIONS

Directions: *In one to three paragraphs, answer the following questions using information from the selection to support your ideas.*

1. After reading this selection, what parallels can you make between the experiences of children learning to speak their first language and international students learning to speak English? Be specific. Give examples.

2. Gestures have different meanings in different cultures. Give an example of a gesture that has one meaning in your culture and another in American culture. Discuss the conflicting messages that these signals send.

3. In your native language, what are the first words children use to refer to their parents? According to the reading, why is it likely that these words are *mama, papa,* or *dada?*

RELATED READINGS

Tangled Tongues and Troubled Tot

About 13 percent of all children have trouble speaking, and for 5 percent the problem is so severe that others cannot understand them. A study of 600 children referred to a speech clinic in Los Angeles found that such children may face the additional burden of psychological problems. Fifty percent (compared with 10 percent in the general population) had emotional or behavioral problems ranging from phobias and separation anxieties to aggressiveness and hyperactivity.

Emotional problems are much less likely among children who had only a speech disorder—difficulty in pronouncing certain sounds—than among those who also had a language disorder—difficulty in expression or comprehension. In a follow-up evaluation four years later, children with speech problems were likely to have lost any psychological problems they may have had, but children with language disorders had more, and more serious, psychological problems, even though their speech and language ability had improved.

"This is just the opposite of what we expected to find," says psycholinguist Lorian Baker, who conducted the study along with child psychiatrist Dennis Cantwell. Both are from the University of California at Los Angeles's Neuropsychiatric Institute. "We had thought that the children with obvious speech difficulties would develop emotional problems from being teased at school. But that wasn't the case. The children with the most serious psychological problems were those who had difficulties in language comprehension, which is much less evident to others."

Baker and Cantwell are continuing their follow-up in an effort to understand the causes. "It could be that language problems cause emotional difficulties, or the other way around, or some third factor may be responsible for both. We just don't know yet," says Baker. But she says she believes that early diagnosis and treatment of speech and language disorders may prevent the development or persistence of psychological problems.

—Beverly McLeod

Out of the Mouths of Babes

How do the meaningless babblings of babies become comprehensible phrases such as "I wanna cookie"? Experts have long agreed that an infant requires some model of human speech, but they have disagreed about its essential features. Psycholinguist Paula Menyuk of Boston University and her colleagues investigated the language development of 56 infants for a three-year period and found that the way a mother talks to her baby does make a difference.

Maternal loquaciousness is not the key; it appears that a talkative model makes no difference in a baby's language development. Rather, the important factor is the number of reasonable opportunities to speak that the mother creates for her child. Infants whose mothers provided them with chances to participate in conversation (called "slots" by Menyuk) developed speaking skills at an earlier age. Mothers create these slots by restating—rather than repeating exactly—what the infant has said, often with rising intonation. For example, if the child says, "I want my blanket," the mother might say, "Your blanket?" or "This blanket?" or "The blue blanket?"

thereby creating a slot for the baby to respond "Yes" or "No."

Similarly, mothers often give what are called proto-directives; they tell the baby to do something while he or she is already doing it. If the child already has teddy bear in hand and appears about to squeeze its stuffing out, the mother might say, "Hug your teddy."

The mothers in Menyuk's study fostered their children's conversational skills by making them a partner in dialogue. They created opportunities for the child to speak and acknowledged the child's attempts at communication, even when such attempts were incomprehensible. They acted as if they were conversing with another person, each taking a turn, and thus created favorable conditions for the child's conversational development.

In order to maintain conversational equity, the mothers fine-tuned their interactions to the child's level of adeptness, asking only what the child was capable of doing. The children in the study had different rates of linguistic development, and mothers adjusted their speech to the child's level at a particular time. Menyuk concludes that mothers' speech to their children is affected by, and at the same time contributes to, the infants' language development.

A manual for parents and clinicians, defining normal language development and describing signs of abnormal development, was written as a result of the study. The monograph, *Prescriptive Manual for Parents and Teachers of Language Impaired Children,* is available from the United States government's Office of Special Education and Rehabilitative Services in Washington, D.C.

—B.M.

—Reprinted with permission from *Psychology Today* Magazine (Sept. 1984): 68–69.
Copyright © 1984 (APA).

DISCUSSION

Directions: Read the following questions. Be prepared to discuss them.

1. How do speech disorders differ from language disorders? Give examples of both.

2. Which is more serious—a language or a speech disorder? Explain your answer.

3. What problems arise when a nonnative speaker of English cannot fully communicate his or her thoughts to native speakers?

4. According to the study, what are different ways that mothers foster the development of their children's conversational skills?

5. Drawing upon information from "Acquisition and Use of Language" as well as from these related articles, explain why you think it isn't sufficient to say that the only way that children learn language is through modeling.

6. As a parent, what are some things you could do to help your young child develop language skills?

Fat Tooth Blues

2

RELATED READING

EAT WELL BUT WISELY

To Reduce Your Risk of Heart Attack

AMERICAN HEART ASSOCIATION

The typical American diet is rich in egg yolks, fatty meats, butter and cream. These are the main sources of cholesterol and animal (saturated) fats. These foods tend to raise the level of cholesterol in the blood, which contributes to the development of atherosclerosis.

Atherosclerosis is a condition in which fatty deposits form on the inner walls of the arteries and interfere with the free flow of blood. Atherosclerosis is the root cause of most heart attacks and strokes.

Most people with a high blood cholesterol level can reduce this risk of heart attack by following a diet designed to control their blood cholesterol levels.

Other ways of reducing the risk of heart attack include maintaining one's proper weight, exercising regularly, getting proper medical treatment for high blood pressure or diabetes, and not smoking cigarettes.

* * *

proteins for animal proteins often. For example, one cup of vegetable proteins such as dried beans, peas or legumes has about as much protein as 2–3 ounces of cooked meat, but contains only a trace of fat. Fish, poultry and veal are low in saturated fat, so eat them more often than beef, lamb or pork.

Choose lean cuts of meat, trim visible fat, and discard the fat that cooks out of the meat.

Avoid frying food; use cooking methods that help remove such fat as baking, boiling, broiling, roasting or stewing.

Restrict your consumption of fatty "luncheon" and "variety" meats like sausages and salami.

Use liquid vegetable oils and margarines rich in polyunsaturated fats instead of butter or other solid cooking fats that are primarily hydrogenated. Select margarines that have liquid vegetable oils such as corn, cottonseed, or sunflower oil listed as their first ingredient.

Use skimmed or low-fat milk and cheeses made from partially skimmed milk instead of whole milk and cheeses made from whole milk and cream.

—Adapted from Eat Well But Wisely. © American Heart Association.

Control Your Intake of Cholesterol-Rich Foods.

Don't eat more than two eggs a week, including those used in cooking, and limit your consumption of shrimp, lobster and organ meats.

Control the Amount and Type of Fat You Eat.

Don't eat more than 5–7 ounces of lean meat, fish, or poultry each day. Substitute vegetable

WE'RE FIGHTING FOR YOUR LIFE

American Heart Association

National Center
7320 Greenville Avenue • Dallas, Texas 75231

DISCUSSION

Directions: Read the following questions. Be prepared to discuss them.

1. This reading is from a pamphlet published by the American Heart Association. What can you guess about the objective of this association?

2. What is the title of this reading? What are the subheadings? What guesses can you make about what this reading will be about?

3. What do you think a healthy diet includes?

4. After skimming the opening paragraphs, complete the chain of events leading to heart attack and stroke.
   a. saturated fat in the diet
   b. _____
   c. _____
   d. _____
   e. _____

5. What are the suggested ways in which people can reduce their risk of heart attack?
   a. _____
   b. _____
   c. _____
   d. _____
   e. _____

6. Considering the content of the selection, put a positive (+) or negative (−) sign next to each of the following foods. Discuss why you marked them as you did.

   _____ oranges   _____ chicken   _____ fish

   _____ chocolate   _____ lobster   _____ ice cream

   _____ bread   _____ rice   _____ carrots

Prereading

DISCUSSION

Directions: Read the following questions. Be prepared to discuss them.

1. What is your definition of a well-balanced meal? What foods are necessary to maintain a well-balanced diet?

2. What is your favorite food? Do you consider it healthy or unhealthy? Why?

3. Americans love to snack. Give examples of "snack foods." What is contained in these foods (vitamins, minerals, etc.)?

4. Are all fats the same? How do they differ? Are some fats healthier than others?

5. What does *Westernization* mean to you? How do you think Westernization affects a society's diet?

6. This article is based on the theory that man has evolved or developed through *evolution*. What does this term mean to you?

PREVIEW

Directions: Read the title and any subheadings of the selection. Also look at the illustrations and read any captions. Then, without reading the selection, answer the following questions.

1. From the title of the selection, what do the following words bring to mind?
   fat
   blues
   deviated
   Stone Age
   What do you expect to be compared?

2. What do the pictures tell you about our ancestors? About their diet? About the accessibility of food? Why do you think that early peoples left drawings of this type?

3. Skim the selection. Then answer the following questions.
   a. What types of fats are discussed?
   b. What aspects of food are important in this selection?
   c. What are some terms used to describe our ancestors?
   d. What specific groups of people are discussed?
   e. What time periods are given?

4. *Hunter-gatherer* is a term used in this selection to describe our ancestors. How do you think these people obtained food? What kind of diet do you think they had?

5. What do you think are the differences in the following terms used to describe the periods of time referred to in this selection?
   prehistoric
   prehuman
   preagricultural

6. Quickly skim the selection again, looking for scientific, historical, or health-related words or terms that you are not familiar with. Write them on a separate piece of paper. As you read the selection, jot down any clues or definitions that will help you understand these words and terms.

READING

FAT TOOTH BLUES

Our diet has deviated dangerously from that of our Stone Age ancestors

S. BOYD EATON AND MARJORIE SHOSTAK

1   A taste for fat, like that for sugar, seems to be part of our human makeup, probably because our primate ancestors ate foods containing these nutrients over tens of millions of years. Fruits, rich in sugar, have been a dietary staple for at least the last twenty-five million years of our evolution, and fat is found in both nuts and meat, items popular with baboons, chimpanzees, and other primates whose omnivorous nature reflects that of our more immediate prehuman ancestors.

2   While fat may have been a taste marker for foods our antecedents relished, under natural circumstances their diet provided fat in relatively small amounts: nuts are typically seasonal and wild game is lean. Beginning in the nineteenth century, however, the food industry began to exploit our taste for fat. Selective breeding and altered feeding practices (including the "finishing" of cattle at feedlots with energy-concentrated corn and grain) have transformed the lean, stringy beef consumed by people in early agricultural societies into tender, juicy, well-marbled beef.

3   Fast-food chains have prospered on fried foods, which multiply the fat content of a base food item: fried shrimp have more than ten

times the fat that boiled shrimp do and French fries have more than eighty times as much fat as do baked potatoes. Many basic foods are now incorporated into pastries, prepared mixes, snack foods, frozen dinners, and other composite items with a much higher fat content, or are garnished with such accompaniments as sour cream, salad dressing, and butter. Children now consume these high-fat foods from their earliest days, so that their tastes are shaped even more to favor and expect such food.

4   The good news is that fat is indispensable to our diets and to eliminate it completely would be harmful. Just as there are essential amino acids—those components of proteins that our bodies cannot synthesize from other dietary constituents—there are essential fatty acids. These are all polyunsaturated, that is, there are at least two double-bond links somewhere in the carbon-atom chain that makes up their backbones. These and similar, mostly polyunsaturated fats are necessary for formation of cell membranes and for synthesis of a variety of structural elements within cells. The body also uses them in the manufacture of prostagladins, specialized hormones that regulate such things as blood pressure, blood clotting, and smooth muscle contraction.

5   The bad news is that—not even counting the extra calories—the kinds and

amounts of fat we eat can hurt our health. There are two other kinds of fats, in addition to polyunsaturated fats. Monounsaturated fats contain one double-bond linkage in their carbon-chain backbones, and saturated fats contain no such double bonds. For many years scientists have known that polyunsaturated fats in the diet tend to lower blood cholesterol levels, though the underlying biochemical mechanism is not fully understood; very recent experimental evidence suggests that monounsaturated fats act similarly. Saturated fats, however, have the opposite effect of increasing the level of blood cholesterol. The higher the cholesterol level, the greater the risk of developing atherosclerosis (hardening of the arteries) and coronary heart disease.

6   Many experimental studies have shown that blood cholesterol levels are lowered in subjects who eat less fat and/or who increase their intake of polyunsaturated fat relative to saturated fat. Cross-cultural studies also find far less coronary heart disease among populations, such as the Japanese and most Third World peoples, that consume little fat generally and tend to eat proportionately more polyunsaturated fat than do Americans.

7   Total fat intake is also related to many cancers (polyunsaturated fats offer no special protection in this regard). In countries where relatively little fat is con-

sumed, cancers of the breast, prostate, uterus, and colon are uncommon or even rare. (Other dietary factors—such as low-fiber diets—may also be implicated, especially in colon cancer.)

8   Fat intake seems related to cancers of the breast, prostate, and uterus because it influences the levels of sex hormones—estrogen in women and testosterone in men. Migration studies show that variation in the incidence of these cancers among groups cannot be explained by genetic differences in susceptibility. For example, ethnic Chinese women living on Taiwan consume little fat, have relatively low levels of estrogenic hormones, and experience little breast cancer; Chinese-American women living in Honolulu consume an intermediate amount of fat, have higher estrogen levels, and a moderate amount of breast cancer; while Chinese-American women living in Boston eat as much fat as do other Bostonians, have relatively high levels of estrogen, and have the same incidence of breast cancer as do white American women. Similarly, black American men eat more fat, have higher testosterone levels, and develop more prostatic cancer than do black Nigerian men.

9   Fat and cancer of the colon are related through a different mechanism. An elevated fat intake stimulates the liver to secrete more bile, which aids in the absorption of fat. When bile

Lean cuisine: Middle Stone Age hunters target an ibex. This 8,000-year-old painting is in Remigia Cave in eastern Spain. (Gallery of Prehistoric Art)

acids pass from the liver into the intestinal tract, they are broken down by microorganisms into substances that are carcinogenic in laboratory animals. The Japanese diet has traditionally contained little fat and the incidence of colon cancer in that country has been very low. As Japan has become more affluent, however, the diet has come to include more fats, and the rate of colon cancer has increased substantially.

10   Compared with animal fat, vegetable fat is less likely to be saturated, and so is often recommended as more healthful. This difference was once less significant. The game our ancestors ate was much leaner than today's domesticated meat:

a venison steak derives 82 percent of its calories from protein and 18 percent from fat, whereas a choice sirloin cut derives 84 percent of its calories from fat and only 16 percent from protein—proportions that are virtually reversed. Meat from free-ranging wild animals also has a much higher proportion of polyunsaturated fat (up to 50 percent) than does supermarket meat (5 percent or less).

11   Why should this be so? First, the vegetation consumed by game animals is higher in polyunsaturated fat than the artificial feed given cattle and pigs. Second, and more important, the excess fat in today's meat animals constitutes reserve energy stores, not structural ele-

ments. Structural fat present in both wild and domesticated animals is largely unsaturated. Storage, or depot, fat (found in layers under the skin, in the marbling of muscle tissue, and within the abdominal cavity) is overwhelmingly saturated. As concentrated sources of energy, these fatty deposits have survival value in times of food shortage. In nature, however, most animals are unable to accumulate anything like the amount of depot fat that our meat animals do as a result of their selective breeding, restricted physical activity, and unnatural diets. Before this century, even domesticated animals lacked the enormous saturated fat deposits we take for granted.

12   The health effects of the fats we eat are influenced by the other foods we consume and by our overall life style. These factors have also changed with time. Nevertheless, the difference between our diet and that of our hunter-gatherer forebears may hold keys to many of our current health problems. The hunting and gathering diet was eaten by all people on earth before the advent of agriculture 10,000 years ago. It was refined over hundreds of thousands—if not millions—of years, as we were evolving. So if there is a diet natural to our human make-up, one to which our genes are still best suited, this is it.

13   A diet now considered balanced includes foods from four major groups: meat, fish, and poultry; breads and cereals; fruits, nuts, and vegetables; and dairy products. People living before the development of agriculture, however, had no dairy foods at all (except mother's milk) and until late in prehistory, made little or no use of grains. Their entire diet was derived from wild game and uncultivated vegetables, and while the proportions of these elements varied widely, we can still make a number of generalizations about the nutrition of these people.

14   First, whether measured by weight or by caloric contribution, plants were probably the staples of diet even before the advent of agriculture, just as they have been for most hunter-gatherers studied by ethnographers. Although animal remains are better preserved in the paleontological record, pollen analysis and the microscopic study of husks, seeds, and other plant remains provide some information about the vegetables, fruits, and nuts consumed. A great variety of plant foods were eaten; in some cases they were brought to living sites from considerable distances.

15   Second, the bulk of carbohydrates consumed in the past were complex, unlike the finely ground flours and refined sugars so abundant in our current diet. Early peoples obtained simple sugars from honey and fruit, but the general absence of dental caries in fossil teeth shows that they ate far fewer sweets than we do. Similarly, their intake of nonnutrient dietary fiber was greater.

16   Third, our forebears ate much more protein, especially animal protein, than we do (and because cholesterol is an integral part of all animal tissue, the amount of cholesterol they ate probably equaled or exceeded what we eat today). The Cro-Magnons, modern humans who lived in Europe between 35,000 and 10,000 years ago, possessed a hunting weaponry so advanced that they could systematically exploit the then plentiful herds of large game animals. The enormous numbers of animal bones found at kill sites and in living areas, as well as the preeminence of animal representations among ancient cave and rock wall paintings left by Cro-Magnons, indicate the importance of meat in their diet.

17   We can ascertain the relative proportions of animal and vegetable food consumed in the past by analyzing skeletal remains. Bones contain both strontium and calcium. Strontium is mostly found in plant foods, so that the bones of herbivores have a higher strontium/calcium ratio than do those of carnivores. Analysis of this ratio in human fossils shows that meat consumption declined just before and during the development of agriculture. Inspection of dental wear patterns, using the scanning electron microscope, tends to confirm this finding.

18   Finally, except for a deficiency of iodine in some geographical locations, our ancestors probably ate an abundance of vitamins and minerals (including calcium —even without any dairy foods). Their intake of potassium, as is the case for all other animals, exceeded their intake of sodium. For most Westernized people thoughout the world, the reverse is now true.

19   Apart from diet, we can assess other features of the Stone Age life style. In isolated locations and in certain seasons, some preagricultural people probably chewed tobacco—as do such modern-day hunters and gatherers as the Australian Aborigines. Tobacco

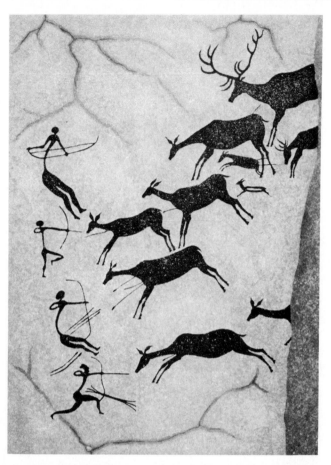

A cave painting from Los Caballos, eastern Spain, depicts the ambush of a deer herd. (Gallery of Prehistoric Art)

was absent from most of the Old World, however, until the European discovery of America, and the New World was not populated until long after the appearance of anatomically modern humans about 40,000 years ago. Smoking almost certainly postdates the advent of agriculture 10,000 years ago, and cigarettes were not even developed until after the Crimean War, in the mid-1850s.

20 As for alcoholic beverages, if preagricultural people had any indigenous brews, these were probably available only seasonally and produced by natural fermentation, not distillation. This would have resulted in drinks of relatively limited potency, beer, for example, as opposed to whiskey. Furthermore, studies of recent hunting and gathering peoples show that among them drinking is subject to strong conventions that limit the frequency and place of consumption, degree of permissible intoxication, and types of behavior that will be tolerated. In such circumstances, the solitary, addictive, pathological drinking found in Western societies is almost nonexistent.

21 Preagricultural hunter-gatherers were also physically fit throughout their lives. We can judge their physical strength directly because we have their skeletal remains. Elevations of dense bone develop where muscle tendons attach to bones. The

size of these elevations reflects the forces generated by the muscles involved. When calibrated in this way, fossil remains show that our remote ancestors possesed great musclar strength, considerably more than is typical of today's Westerners.

22   Fossil bones show that ancestral peoples were not only strong but also tall. The Cro-Magnons were slightly taller than present-day Americans. More impressive, the 1984 discovery of a nearly complete fossilized skeleton of *Homo erectus*—a more remote human ancestor— showed that people living as much as 1.6 million years ago were equal to us in height. The usual assumption has been that our ancestors were all smaller than we were.

23   These findings can be broadened by examining the life style of contemporary peoples who live by hunting and gathering, such as the !Kung and ≠Kade San (Bushmen) of Botswana, the Pygmies of Zaire, the Australian Aborigines, and the Arctic Eskimos. There are important differences between these people and our Stone Age ancestors. Contemporary hunters and gatherers inhabit ecologically marginal desert, jungle, or arctic regions where the food quest must be more difficult than it was for people living 25,000 years ago in richer locales. Most such groups are technologically more advanced than their Stone Age predecessors (even the

ubiquitous bow and arrow is relatively new, appearing no earlier than 20,000 years ago), and virtually all have had considerable contact with the outside world. Nevertheless, many of the constraints operating on the hunting and gathering life in the past continue to shape this way of life today.

24   Studies of more than fifty such groups during this century reveal that their average (and most common) nutritional pattern is based on about 35 percent meat and 65 percent vegetable food, by weight. The range is considerable, from 90 percent meat in the Arctic to less than 15 percent in arid deserts. (The relative proportions in Western cultures are difficult to assess because so many of our foods are amalgamations of vegetable and animal products.)

25   Americans currently obtain between 40 and 45 percent of their daily calories from fat, and of this, twice as much is saturated as is polyunsaturated. Among hunter-gatherers, only about 20 percent of daily caloric intake is derived from fat, and of this, more is polyunsaturated than is saturated. (The Eskimos, an extreme case, traditionally obtained about 40 percent of their calories from fat, but this was high in polyunsaturated fat.) Cross-cultural differences were part of the evidence taken into account when the Senate Select Committee on Nutrition issued its Dietary Goals in

1978. These recommended that fat should provide 30 percent of American caloric needs, divided equally among saturated, monounsaturated, and polyunsaturated fat.

26   Aside from lower total fat intake and lower proportions of saturated to polyunsaturated fat, hunter-gatherer diets reflect other principles that American medical organizations recommend: little salt, few refined sugars, high fiber, moderate (although adequate) calories, and a wide range of complex carbohydrates.

27   The hunting and gathering life style also involves considerable physical exercise, begun in early childhood and continued throughout life. Much of this is highly aerobic, promoting stamina comparable to that achieved in our society only by accomplished endurance athletes. Careful epidemiological investigations show that such aerobic fitness promotes health by reducing blood pressure and by protecting against atherosclerosis. Exertion in tasks requiring physical strength, also typical of hunter-gatherers, toughens bones and supporting tissues around joints, thus minimizing the risk of osteoporosis and excessive damage from trauma.

28   As a result of their life style, contemporary hunter-gatherers are healthier than we are, at least with regard to those "diseases of civilization"—heart attack, cancer, stroke, hypertension, obesity,

and diabetes—that cause most deaths in affluent Western nations. They do not suffer from atherosclerosis, which predisposes us toward coronary heart disease. This is because they are not exposed to cigarettes, eat relatively little fat (with a beneficial ratio of polyunsaturated to saturated fat), and generally maintain a high level of aerobic fitness. A diet low in sodium but containing ample potassium and calcium keeps their blood pressures constant over the years (ours tend to rise with age), and they experience little or no hypertension.

29   Thanks to the strenuous physical activity required by their lives and to a moderate caloric intake (their foods aren't calorically concentrated, as ours often are), hunter-gatherers are almost never obese and have exceptionally low rates of diabetes. Unfortunately we know little about cancer among foraging peoples, because biopsy and autopsy data are generally unavailable. Studies among the Eskimos, however, have found that the incidence of cancer has increased significantly following Westernization.

30   It is not because individuals in industrialized countries live longer that they are afflicted by the diseases of civilization. Young people in the Western world commonly harbor developing, asymptomatic forms of these various conditions, whereas hunter-gatherer youth do

not. Furthermore, those members of foraging cultures who live to age sixty and beyond remain free from these diseases, in striking contrasts with persons of similiar age who live in Western nations.

31   This should not suggest that hunting-gathering societies are, over all, healthier than our own, because conditions we are able to control (such as infections and trauma) often cause the early death of their members. But their life style does protect hunter-gatherers from the diseases that kill most of us. By picking and choosing the best from their life style along with the best from ours, we should be able to forestall (or even prevent) many currently prominent diseases and thus live longer, healthier lives.

32   The diseases attributed by medical and epidemiological research to excessive dietary fat appear to represent chronic derangements of basic biological processes—metabolic pathways that evolution has conserved and that are functionally similiar to those of other mammals, of vertebrates generally, and even, in some case, of unicellular organisms. These diseases differ completely from the infections and traumas that were the chief causes of death before this century.

33   The amount and type of fat we consume represent new and exceptional metabolic circumstances—ones

that have previously challenged few humans (or, for that matter, other animals). Our genes cannot have adapted in any significant way to this particular challenge. The glacial pace of genetic evolution is indicated by evidence that the genes of humans and chimpanzees differ by only about 1.5 percent, even though our ancestors diverged from theirs about seven million years ago. The novel but widespread phenonmenon of excessive fat intake (and particularly our heavy load of saturated fat) is, over an entire life span, incompatible with our genetically determined physiology and biochemistry. The resultant mismatch promotes diseases that, taken together, cause more than half the deaths in the United States today.

S. Boyd Eaton, M.D., is chief of radiology at West Paces Ferry Hospital in Atlanta, associate clinical professor of radiology at Emory University Medical School, and adjunct associate professor of anthropology at Emory University. Majorie Shostak, the author of Nisa: The Life and Words of a !Kung Woman, *is research associate in anthropology at the Graduate Institute of Liberal Arts at Emory University. With coauthor Melvin Konner, Eaton and Shostak are writing a book on the continuing importance of the hunting and gathering adaptation to human life today. Tentatively titled* The Paleolithic Prescription, *1988, Harper and Row.*

—With permission from *Natural History*, Vol. 95, No. 7; copyright the American Museum of Natural History, 1986.

Postreading

TRUE OR FALSE

Directions: Decide if each of the following statements is true (T) or false (F) based on the selection.

_____ **1.** Our taste for fat and sugar appears to have stemmed from our prehuman ancestors.

_____ **2.** The content of beef has changed very little since prehistoric times.

_____ **3.** Polyunsaturated fats as well as saturated fats help to lower blood cholestrol levels.

_____ **4.** Polyunsaturated fats differ from one another in the number of double-bond units in their carbon chains.

_____ **5.** Saturated fats are linked to atherosclerosis and coronary heart disease.

_____ **6.** Polyunsaturated fats guard against high cholesterol levels and various types of cancer.

_____ **7.** Animal fat contains more saturated fat than does vegetable fat.

_____ **8.** The meat we now consume contains high proportions of structured fats, which for the most part are unsaturated.

_____ **9.** Although our ancestors lacked many of the agricultural skills we have today, their diet appears to have been healthier than ours.

_____ **10.** Preagricultural people are compared to present day hunter-gatherers because of their similarities in diet and lifestyle.

_____ **11.** Analysis of our ancestors' bones has revealed that these people obtained most of their protein from vegetables.

_____ **12.** Tobacco and alcohol were never used in preagricultural societies.

READING WORKSHEET

Directions: After you have completed the true-or-false exercise, answer the following questions. You may refer to the selection if necessary.

1. Choose the best paraphrase for the first sentence in paragraph 1.
   a. It appears that the desire to eat sweets and fat exists because our primate ancestors consumed foods containing fats and sugars.
   b. We can taste fat and sugar in the foods that we eat because people millions of years ago began to eat sweet and fatty foods.
   c. Fat and sugar have made up a large part of the human diet for millions of years because our primate ancestors liked the taste.

2. What does *our antecedents* refer to in the first sentence of paragraph 2? _____

3. What is the main idea of paragraph 3?
   a. Many basic foods have been transformed into very fatty foods, which we have learned to love.
   b. Children are eating a lot of fatty foods.
   c. We develop a taste for fatty foods at a very early age.

4. Paragraph 4 gives us the "good news," then, paragraph _____ gives us the "bad news."

   Good news: (paraphrase your answer) _____

   _____

   Bad news: (paraphrase) _____

   _____

5. Locate the following pronouns in paragraph 4: *it*, *there*, and *them*. What do each of these pronouns refer to?

   a. _____

   b. _____

   c. _____

6. In paragraph 5, why do you think the phrase *not even counting*

the extra calories is set off by dashes? _____

_____

7. What is atherosclerosis? How does the author signal its definition?

_____

8. In paragraph 6, the results of cross-cultural studies are discussed. Keeping these results in mind, describe what you think a cross-cultural study is. _____

_____

9. What is the relationship that is implied between fat consumption and the cancers listed in paragraph 7? _____

_____

10. Reread the information about migration studies. Keeping in mind the information that was discovered through these studies, describe what you think a migration study might be. _____

_____

What two migration studies are described? _____

_____

What theory does the information in these two studies support?

_____

11. In paragraph 9, the authors use factual information to support a theory.
Theory: _____

Supporting evidence: _____

12. Paragraph 11 begins with a question. What is the function of this question? _____

What does the word *this* in the question refer to? _____

What are the two answers to this question? _____

_____

13. What are the four major food groups? _____

_____

How are the divisions between these groups shown? _____

14. The purpose of paragraph 13 is to
   a. act as a transition between paragraphs 12 and 14.
   b. introduce a new topic.
   c. describe a balanced diet.

15. The last sentence in paragraph 13 is used as a topic sentence for
the following _____ paragraphs. How many "generalizations"
are made in the next few paragraphs? _____ What are these
generalizations? _____

_____

_____

_____

16. What does the word *similarly* mean in paragraph 15? _____

_____

17. What does *this finding* in the last sentence of paragraph 17 refer to?

_____

18. The last sentence in paragraph 18 states that "the reverse is true."
What does *the reverse* refer to? _____

_____

19. In paragraph 18, what do the phrases *in isolated locations* and *in
certain seasons* tell us about Stone Age people's use of tobacco?

_____

20. Who do the authors compare Australian Aborigines to? _____

21. Choose the best paraphrase of the last two sentences in paragraph 20.
   a. Alcoholism was probably virtually unknown in prehistoric
   societies because studies of similar groups of people show that

circumstances of drinking and permissible drunken behaviors
are in some way regulated among such groups.
  b. Studies show that ancient peoples probably didn't drink much
  because it was against their cultural values.
  c. Drinking is limited to agricultural societies because of regulations
  concerning when, where, and what to drink, whereas alcoholism
  is unknown in Western societies.

22. Paragraph 21 posits a theory in its topic sentence.

    Theory: _____

    What evidence is used to support this theory? _____

    _____

23. What "groups" are being referred to in paragraph 24? _____

24. Look at the information about Eskimos in paragraph 25. Are Es-
    kimos an example of Americans or hunter-gatherers? _____

25. What does *Aside from* mean in paragraph 26?
    a. In addition to
    b. However
    c. In contrast to

26. In paragraph 27, are the authors referring to present-day hunter-
    gatherers or the hunter-gatherers of 25,000 years ago? _____

    How do you know about whom they are talking? _____

27. What are "the diseases of civilization" referred to in para-
    graph 28? _____

28. Locate the phrase *hunter-gatherer youth do not* (paragraph 30). Do
    not what?

    _____

29. Reread the last sentence in paragraph 30. It is a sentence of contrast
    stating that the older members of "foraging cultures" do not suffer
    from "these diseases."

    What are "foraging cultures"? _____

What are "these diseases"? _____

What does this sentence imply about persons from Western nations?

(Keep in mind that the sentence is one of contrast.) _____

_____

30. What is the "mismatch" discussed in paragraph 33? _____

_____

31. Locate the word *glacial* in paragraph 33. The noun form of this word is *glacier*. If you don't know the meaning of this word, look it up in the dictionary. Now, thinking about the way a glacier moves,

what synonyms can you suggest for *glacial pace*? _____

_____

INFERENCE AND RESTATEMENT

Directions: *Decide whether each of the following is a restatement (R), an inference (I), or a false statement (F) according to the selection. If the sentence is a restatement, locate the original in the selection and give the paragraph number where it is found.*

_____ **1.** The typical American diet contains much more fat than our bodies need.

_____ **2.** The diets of prehistoric people did not contain fat.

_____ **3.** Animal fats tend to raise the amount of cholesterol in the blood, while fats from vegetable sources tend to lower it.

_____ **4.** People should not eat large quantities of fat because of the increased risk of certain types of cancer.

_____ **5.** Even though people in developing countries experience lower rates of many types of cancer, studies show that this is not due to genetic factors.

_____ **6.** People in other countries are safe from diseases related to high-fat diets.

_____ **7.** Dairy products are essential to a healthy diet.

_____ **8.** If we look at the fossil remains of prehistoric people, we can guess the ratio of meat to vegetables in their diets.

_____ **9.** Close to one half of the calories in the typical American diet comes from fat.

_____**10.** The diet and physical activity of our ancestors prevented them from becoming obese.

OUTLINING

Directions: *Below is a partial outline of paragraphs 13 through 18. Reread the section and complete this outline.*

Paragraphs 13 through 18 discuss the nutritional aspects of prehistoric peoples. Locate the thesis for this discussion. Write it here.

I. _____

_____

(As you might have already guessed, we are writing primarily a sentence outline. Use a complete sentence for main/major supporting ideas. You may use noun phrases for examples.)

According to the topic sentence you gave in I above, what are the generalizations being made? (List in A, B, C, and D.)

    A. Plants were probably the staples of diet.

        1. A great variety of plant foods were eaten.

            a) _____

            b) _____

            c) _____

    B. _____

        1. _____

            a) Honey

            b) _____

        2. _____

        3. They consumed a greater amount of nonnutrient dietary fiber than we do.

    C. _____

    1. The Cro-Magnons _____

    2. _____ was important in their diet.

       a) Enormous numbers of animal bones have been found.

       b) _____

    3. Meat consumption declined _____.

       a) A conclusion has been made through _____.

          (1) Bones contain _____ and _____.

          (2) Strontium is found _____.

             (a) Herbivores have _____.

             (b) _____

D. _____

    1. There was a deficiency _____.

    2. Their intake of _____.

Vocabulary from Context

Direction: _Using your own knowledge and information from the text, answer the following questions. Refer to the selection while you work. Don't be afraid to guess._

  1. primate (paragraph 1)
In this paragraph, examples of some primates are given. What are these examples? _____

    Primate means _____.

  2. antecedents (paragraph 2)
Read the sentence containing this term. Find a synonym in paragraph 1.

    Antecedent (in this context) means _____.

  3. relished (paragraph 2)
Notice the transition word used in this sentence. What is it?
_____ What type of relationship does it show between the

clauses? _____ Also read what the next sentence says about how we feel about fat.

Relish means _____.

4. indispensable (paragraph 4)
   Read the sentence. Notice the connector and think about how the two clauses are related

   Indispensable means _____.

5. domesticated (paragraph 10)
   Notice the comparison made in this sentence between "game" (which our ancestors ate) and "domesticated" meat (which we eat). Also notice that examples of each are given later in the sentence.

   Domesticated means _____.

6. deficiency (paragraph 18)
   The sentence containing this word sets up an opposite relationship between the amount of iodine and the amounts of other vitamins and minerals in the diet by using the phrase *except for*. What is the

   opposite of deficiency? _____

   Deficiency means _____.

Summary

Directions: Write a summary of the selection. Include as many of the following words and phrases (or their related forms) as you wish. Begin with this sentence: Human beings have always had a taste for fat.

Western countries   dairy products
prehistoric ancestors   migration studies
animal sources
plant sources
domesticated animals
free-ranging animals
heart disease
cancer
grains

ESSAY QUESTIONS

Directions: In one to three paragraphs, answer the following questions using information from the selection to support your ideas.

1. The authors make no specific suggestions for improving the health of people who eat a modern Western diet. What changes in lifestyle and diet would you recommend?

2. What evidence do the authors offer to support the idea that cancer, heart disease, and diabetes really aren't diseases of old age? How is this idea important in a society where the average person lives to be seventy years old?

3. How does your personal diet compare to the typical Western diet described in the selection? What changes could you make in your own diet and lifestyle to improve your health?

3 | Cancer: Cells Out of Control

Prereading

DISCUSSION

Directions: Read the following questions. Be prepared to discuss them.

1. What kind of information does every package of cigarettes carry? What harmful ingredients do cigarettes contain?

2. What warnings are given for some types of sugarless gum or sugarless soda? What possibly harmful ingredient(s) do these foods contain? Why are these warnings written on packages?

3. Why can sunbathing be dangerous?

4. What thoughts does the word *cancer* bring to mind?

5. What are some common types of cancer and what are their suspected causes?

Cancer	Causes
_____	_____
_____	_____
_____	_____

6. Who do you believe is most likely to get cancer? Males? Females? Young? Old? People living in certain regions? People of certain races?

PREVIEW

Directions: Read the title and any subheadings of the selection. Also look at the illustrations and read any captions. Then, without reading the selection, answer the following questions.

1. What is the definition of cancer?

   _____

   Where is this found? _____

   _____

2. How many major sections are there? _____ How are these sec-

tions divided? _____ Write the heading for each:

3.1 _____

3.2 _____

From this information, answer the following questions:

a. How many kinds of carcinogens are there? _____

b. What are these carcinogens? _____

_____

3. How are key words emphasized? _____

What kind of information do you think may follow these key words?

_____

4. What does Figure 3–1 show?

a. _____

b. _____

5. According to Figure 3–3, who dies more often from cancer, men

or women? _____

6. Notice the last sentence in paragraph 1. What is the form of this

sentence? _____

What is its purpose? _____

This type of sentence is a rhetorical device. Locate other places in
the reading where rhetorical questions are used. Write the sentences
below.

_____

_____

READING

CANCER: CELLS OUT OF CONTROL

3–1 What Is Cancer?

1   Cancer is a ubiquitous killer. World-wide, 2 million people each year die of cancer, and in the United States more than 250,000 deaths are annually attributed to this disease. In morbidity statistics for the United States, cancer ranks second as the principal disease causing death, surpassed in importance only by the cardiovascular diseases. It has been estimated that about 50,000 person-years are lost annually because of disabilities caused by cancer and $12 billion are lost yearly in goods and services. Cancer is indiscriminate; it affects young and old, male and female, rich and poor. What is cancer and how can it be recognized?

2   One of the inherited tendencies of living matter is to multiply. Cellular growth and multiplication are dynamic processes, but in our bodies such events are under some sort of restraining influence; unchecked or unlimited cell division ordinarily does not occur. For example, if a wound is made in the skin, let us say a cut, some striking changes in the pattern of cell growth take place (Figure 3–1a). The cells that surround the gaping wound detach themselves, become ameboid, and move into the wound area; on the way, these cells begin to divide. The cells continue the process of division until the entire wound is filled. Now cell touches neighboring cell, the proliferation of cells ceases,

and the wound is healed. Similarly, when a tissue or an organ is in the process of growing, the cells multiply, but once a certain size is reached the multiplication process ceases.

3   Suppose a few of our skin cells, especially those that divide to replace the cells continually being lost at the surface, escape from controlling factors and the daughter cells continue to multiply; eventually a cluster of cells is produced (Figure 3–1b). Similar uncontrolled cell division in any part of the body could result in an abnormal, functionless lump or mass of cells—a **cancer** or **tumor** (the terms are synonymous). The cancer cell is often described as being **neoplastic** (*neos—new; plasma*—a thing formed; Gk.), since it has been transformed from a cellular condition of rest with the synthetic machinery turned off to a condition of continuous growth and multiplication.[1] Cancer cells contribute nothing to the tissue from which they arose; they often interfere with and damage neighboring normal cells and monopolize the food supply.

4   To most people cancers are "rampant, predatory, savage, ungovernable, greedy cells—flesh destroying itself." To a biologist, the cancer cell is one with an inherited capacity for autonomous growth, that is, it determines its own activities irrespective of the laws that precisely regulate the growth of all normal cells. To a clin-

Source: From *Biology: A Human Approach,* Third Edition, by Irwin W. Sherman and Vilia G. Sherman. Copyright © 1975, 1979, 1983 by Oxford University Press, Inc. Reprinted by permission.

[1]The time spent in mitosis by a cancer cell is the same as that of normal cells, but the frequency of cell division is greater for the cancer cell.

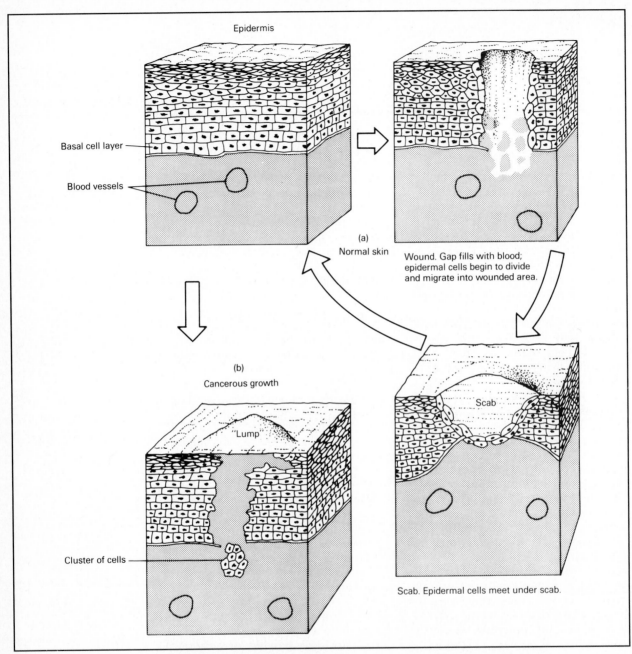

Epidermis

Basal cell layer

Blood vessels

(a)
Normal skin

Wound. Gap fills with blood; epidermal cells begin to divide and migrate into wounded area.

(b)
Cancerous growth

"Lump"

Cluster of cells

Scab

Scab. Epidermal cells meet under scab.

FIGURE 3–1. Patterns of skin growth. (a) Wound healing. (b) Cancer.

ical physician, a cancer is a malignancy that is ultimately lethal. The clinical physician distinguishes tumors, or cancers, by their appearance and their manner of distribution, designating them as **benign** (harmless) or **malignant** (deadly). The property of autonomy is expressed in both benign and malignant tumors; how then do they differ from one another?

5 Normal cells of the body tend to respond to the presence of abnormal objects such as tumors by attempting to surround them in an envelope of tissue, thus isolating them and cutting them off from the rest of the body. If a tumor is surrounded by a connective-tissue capsule and is thus restricted in its growth, it is called a benign, or harmless, tumor (Figure 3–2a). Of themselves, benign tumors do not kill, but they can interfere with normal function; for example, they can obstruct the bowel. Benign tumors can be cured because they can be removed by surgical means; warts are examples of benign tumors, caused by a virus.

6 Sometimes benign tumors give rise to another kind, called an **invasive tumor.** In such a condition the normal tissue cannot keep pace with the rapidly dividing cancer cells, and the capsule breaks down. The cancer cells break out of the connective-tissue capsule, grow outside the capsule, and infiltrate the surrounding tissues (Figure 3–2b). Such a condition is more difficult to handle and may cause a diseased condition; this is a malignant tumor. The malignant invasive tumor may eventually become surrounded by blood vessels and lymphatics; the tumor, or cancer, cells may then enter these vessels and be transported to other parts of the body (Figure 3–2c). This is a malignant **metastatic tumor** and is extremely difficult to treat by surgical procedures. The cancer cells may eventually lodge in the lungs, liver, or kidney or be held in the lymph nodes; there they may proliferate and cause further damage and destruction to the vital organs of the body. Whole-body treatment with drugs or irradiation must be instituted to control such a malignant metastatic cancer.

7 It is apparent from this discussion that the cancer cell differs from ordinary normal cells in its relationship with neighboring body cells. Ordi-

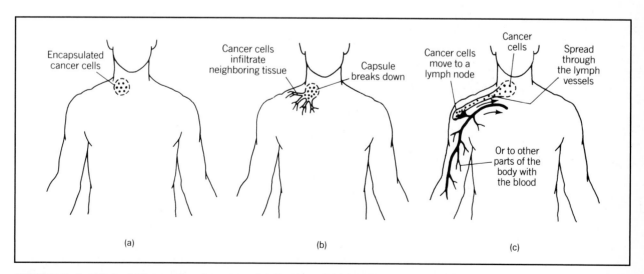

FIGURE 3–2. Clinical diagnosis of cancer. (a) Benign. (b) Invasive. (c) Metastatic.

narily, normal cells are confined with specific tissues and maintain themselves in a precise and orderly architectural pattern; the cancer cell does not remain confined to the tissue from which it originated, but moves into the surrounding tissues and there continues its proliferative ways. Many cancers show this invasive tendency, and in this way they "claw" their way through the body, injuring and killing other cells. To the early physicians who first observed these cellular tendencies, the hardened body of tumor tissue resembled the body of a crab and the rapidly dividing cancer cells projecting out of this mass and invading surrounding tissues appeared like the crab's claws; it was imaginative, if perhaps not quite logical, to call the disease "cancer" after the Greek word *karkinos*, meaning "crab."

3–2. Carcinogens: Cancer-Causing Agents

8   Agents capable of causing cancer are called **carcinogens;** they come from a variety of sources and can be classified into three basic groups: chemical, physical, and viral.

Chemical Agents

9   **Occupational.** The first occupational cancer caused by a chemical was described in 1775 by the English physician Percival Pott as "a scrotal cancer of chimney sweeps." The frequency of skin cancer, particulary in the area of the scrotum, was greater in sweeps who had started as climbing boys early in childhood, yet the symptoms appeared only in sweeps who had been in the profession for 20 years or more. Pott surmised that the tumors had originated from soot which accumulated and persisted longer in the scrotal region because of poor hygiene. The clinical observation of the relationship between soot and scrotal cancer resulted in a set of safety regulations, in the form of bathing requirements. As a result, the incidence of scrotal cancer among sweeps showed a sharp decrease. It was not until 150 years later that Pott's clinical observations were confirmed experimentally. In 1932, Kennaway and his colleagues isolated a specific chemical from coal tar, 3:4-benzpyrene, and this alone induced cancerous lesions.

10   Workers in the dye industry show a high incidence of bladder cancer, and the carcinogen involved is β-naphthylamine, which is used as the starting material for the synthesis of many dyestuffs. Petroleum workers, too, show a higher incidence of cancers than the general populace, but the agents involved have not yet been identified. Asbestos, nickel, uranium, chromates, and arsenic have all been shown to be involved in cancerous lesions.

11   **Dietary.** Recent evidence indicates that we are surrounded by numerous dietary agents that may be carcinogenic. A potent carcinogen popularly known as "butter yellow" (*N*-dimethylaminobenzene) used to be routinely added to butter to make it more yellow and presumably more attractive to the consumer; fortunately, the quantity used for coloring was quite low and the practice has now been prohibited. Certain other food additives, such as cyclamates and saccharin, have been implicated in bladder cancer in mice, and older case studies showed that the hormone diethylstilbestrol, used for

caponizing fowl, could also produce animal cancers. Dietary factors in some countries are associated with or implicated in cancer of the esophagus and the stomach. In Ceylon and India, cancers of the mouth and throat are common and are related to the habit of chewing mixtures of tobacco, betel nut, and lime. The evidence at present, as with most cancer research on humans, is strictly statistical, but diet itself does represent a potential source of carcinogens.

12   **Hormonal.** Within our own bodies there may be agents potentially capable of inducing cancer. Particularly suspect is the female hormone estrogen. Long-term application of estrogen to the skin has caused cancers in experimental animals, and the continued application of estrogen in guinea pigs causes uterine tumors; mice can be induced to produce pituitary tumors by estrogen administration. For humans, the effects of hormones on cancer development are not as clear-cut, but recent evidence indicates that women taking the contraceptive pill show a higher incidence of breast and uterine cancer than women who do not take it; the pill contains synthetic steroids that have effects similar to those of estrogen and progesterone. In men under treatment with estrogen it is not unusual to find an enlargement of the breasts, and some of these show precancerous lesions. It is suspected, but by no means proved, that estrogen may play a significant role in the development of certain forms of cancer.

13   **Atomospheric Pollution.** Whenever hydrocarbons such as gasoline, coal, oil, gas, or other fuels are incompletely burned, a variety of compounds are produced that have been identified as carcinogenic. In the at-mosphere over most large cities, a dense blanket of air pollutants causes eye irritation, difficulty in breathing, and a range of other discomforts. In every month in every square mile of Manhattan more than 1,520 lb. of tar settle down, a small fraction of the 176 tons of solids that rain down on the inhabitants each month. The soot of the air contains the powerful carcinogen 3:4-benzpyrene, and the amount of that chemical increases during the winter with increased burning of fossil fuels. The frequency of lung cancer is directly related to the density of the population, indicating that atmospheric pollution may play a significant role. With continued increase in population and an increased utilization of fossil fuels, there seems little doubt that the larger amounts of carinogens produced will enhance the incidence of cancer.

14   **Smoking and Lung Cancer.** At the present time, the side panel of every package of cigarettes manufactured in the United States carries the statement "Warning: The Surgeon General Has Determined That Cigarette Smoking Is Dangerous to Your Health." Much experimental evidence for a variety of laboratory animals indicates that inhaled cigarette smoke can be carcinogenic. Cigarette smoke contains 6,800 different chemicals, several of which (dimethylnitrosamine, hydrazine, and vinyl chloride) have been shown in animal tests to be powerful carcinogens. For example, in experiments where dogs smoked cigarettes and extracts from cigarette smoke were painted on the backs of mice, tumors developed. Critics of these tests maintain that the results cannot be extrapolated to humans. They may be correct, but continually accumulating evidence indicates that

the critics are probably wrong. No direct experiments using cigarette-smoke carcinogens can be performed on humans, and so the evidence is primarily statistical. Be that as it may, the statistics show that smoking is hazardous to one's health.

15   If the incidence of lung cancer in England is plotted against the increased cigarette consumption, then it is clearly seen that the rise in deaths due to cancer follows that nation's cigarette consumption (Figure 3–3). Also, because of social habits, the rise in lung cancer increased in men long before it did in women.

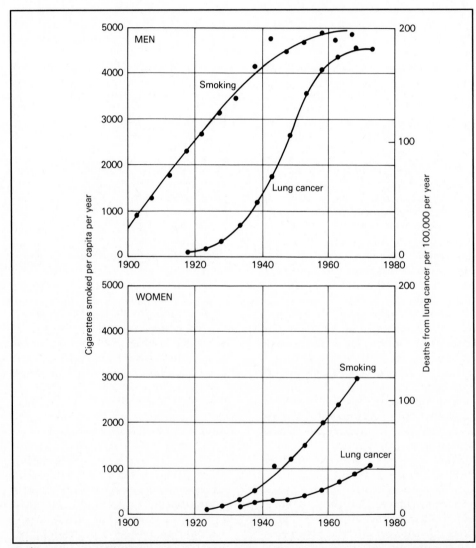

FIGURE 3–3. Relation between smoking and subsequent rise in the death rate from lung cancer for men and women in England. (After Royal College of Physicians, Smoking and Health Now)

Notice also that there is about a 20-year interval between the time people begin to smoke and the measurable increase in lung cancer.

16 If every smoker in America stopped smoking today, hundreds of thousands of premature deaths from a variety of cancers could be prevented. Since such warnings are likely to go unheeded, we can expect 100,000 persons to die annually from lung cancer alone; more persons will die from lung cancer than from automobile accidents!

17 The longer an individual smokes, the greater the possibility of developing lung cancer. The most important factor in the development of lung cancer is that the risk increases with the amount of smoke inhaled and the duration of the smoking habit. Cigarette smoking also bears a causal relationship to other disorders, such as Buerger's disease (an inflammation of the arteries), emphysema, chronic bronchitis, and heart disease. These correlations do not prove a cause-and-effect relationship, but they do suggest a strong link between the smoking of cigarettes, cancer, and related diseases.

18 Over the last 40 years, overwhelming evidence has accumulated that Americans, and others elsewhere around the world, are increasingly filling their environment with carcinogenic chemicals. The World Health Organization currently estimates that environmental agents are responsible for more than 75 percent of human cancers. A National Cancer Institute map shows the areas of the United States with the highest death rates from lung, liver, and bladder cancer . . . are the same regions that have the greatest amount of chemical pollution. Yet there is hope: if the main causes of cancer are indeed environmental, then potentially this disease could be prevented (Box 3A).

Physical Carcinogens

19 **Ultraviolet Light and Skin Cancer.** One of the diversions considered fashionable in modern society is to lie in the radiant sunshine for hours at a time, covered with some kind of greasy substance; at the end of this time the sunbather hopes to have acquired a deep brown suntan. The effect of the sun's ultraviolet light upon the skin of most humans is to produce first a redness that may be accompanied by a soreness; then if the dose is not severe enough to cause blistering and peeling, the red fades and is replaced by a brown coloration—the much desired tan. The redness is produced by the dilation of blood vessels creating increased blood flow in the area, and the skin becomes red and warm. In the tanning process, ultraviolet light causes the deeper layers to produce the pigment melanin which migrates to the more superficial layers (Figure 3–4). If the skin is not reexposed, the tan fades. In many respects the effect of ultraviolet light represents a type of inflammation, and commonly there is some damage to the skin cells. Such injury results not only in the elaboration of melanin but in the thickening of the skin itself by a proliferation of cells and a greater deposition of keratin.[2] Does this ultraviolet-light-induced aging and cellular proliferation eventually lead to cancer? There is some uncertainty and doubt regarding this question, but certain factors suggest that this may indeed be the case. It is estimated that 10 per-

[2]Microscopic examination of skin from the face and arms of fair-skinned but overtanned individuals shows that the cells resemble those taken from the skin of very old men and women (cells from unexposed areas such as the buttocks retained a youthful appearance). Sunburning and suntanning tend to age the skin prematurely.

Box 3A The cancer screen

Medical scientists have been trying for decades to identify those chemicals that are carcinogenic. That task is not easily accomplished. During a lifetime we are exposed to literally millions of chemical compounds, both natural and synthetic. To screen each of these compounds for their carcinogenic properties would require extensive animal testing, involving many years and costing millions. However, there may be a way to speed up the process. A simple and inexpensive cancer screening test was developed by Bruce Ames, a biochemist at the University of California. The **Ames test** is based on the theory that carcinogens damage nucleic acids, causing mutations and thereby inducing cancer. Bacteria do not get cancer but are vulnerable to mutations. Ames used a mixture of four mutants of the bacterium *Salmonella typhimurium* that were unable to make the amino acid histidine; such mutants do not grow unless histidine is added to the agar on which they are placed. When exposed to agents causing mutations **(mutagens),** these strains may mutate further; some of these mutations, by chance, will repair the original genetic defect, making their possessor normal. If this occurs, the bacteria will grow on agar containing no histidine and colonies will form on the agar surface. The colonies show up as white dots and can easily be counted. The more powerful the mutagen, the more colonies there are that will grow in the absence of histidine. Thus, colony numbers give some measure of the potency of the mutagenic agent. Of 174 known carcinogens tested, 157 (90 percent) were mutagenic in the Ames test. Out of a group of 180 so-called noncarcinogens, 14 were mutagenic. Some of these mutagens may well cause cancer. For example, a food additive called furylfuramide that was used in Japan for 8 years had been shown to be noncarcinogenic in animal tests; however, recent studies show it to be both mutagenic and carcinogenic. Furylfuramide is positive in the Ames test.

All evidence indicates that certain chemicals and radiation in the environment damage DNA; over a lifetime this cumulative damage is probably the cause of most human cancers. The Ames mutagenicity test is a cheap way of determining whether a chemical compound is likely to be dangerous to humans. It may also enable us to tell whether an individual who has been exposed to a suspected carcinogen is carrying a lethal time bomb within her or him. A physician suspicious of such a condition could take a sample of the patient's urine, add it to a culture of *Salmonella*, and see if it is mutagenic. If detected early, treatment could be initiated. Mutagenic screening could make it possible to protect the public against hazardous substances before and not after they have been in widespread use.

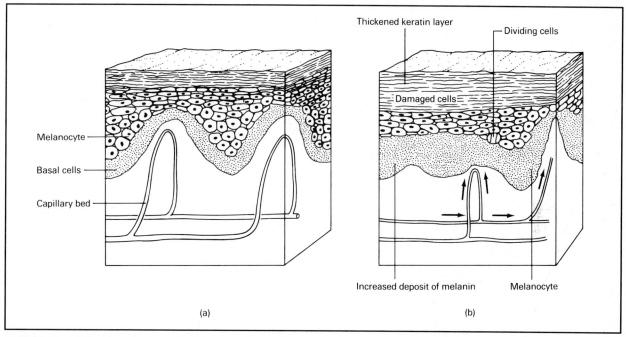

Thickened keratin layer

Dividing cells

Damaged cells

Melanocyte

Basal cells

Capillary bed

Increased deposit of melanin

Melanocyte

(a)   (b)

FIGURE 3–4. Changes in the skin induced by sunburn. (a) Before sunburn. (b) After sunburn, there is increased blood flow in the capillary bed (arrows), greater deposition of melanin, death of epidermal cells, increased cell division, and a thickening of the keratin layer.

cent of human cancers are related to exposure to ultraviolet rays; most of these are cancers of the skin, and 95 percent of such cancers are curable if treated in time—while they are still benign and before they metastasize. Skin cancers occur more frequently on the parts of the body that are habitually exposed to sunlight, skin cancer is more prevalent among populations dwelling in the sunnier regions of the globe, and skin cancer appears more frequently in light-skinned than in dark-skinned persons and more frequently among outdoor than indoor workers. Mice can be induced to produce skin cancers by treatment with low doses of ultraviolet light for 5 days a week over 161 days; human beings have 70 years or so for exposure and therefore a greater likelihood of de-

veloping skin cancer (the life-span of a mouse is about 2 years). If the effects of sunlight are cumulative as experiments with mice suggest, the risk of skin cancer in humans due to the effects of the sunlight increases with age and is very great indeed.

X Radiation.   X rays are much more energetic than ultraviolet rays and, as one would expect, are much more effective in producing skin cancer. The early radiologists, unaware of the carcinogenic effects of x rays, developed severe carcinomas of the hands after repeated brief exposures to low doses of x rays. The frequency of leukemia among radiologists is ten times greater than among other physicians. The leukemia incidence among the survivors of Nagasaki and Hiroshima is five times that of the rest of the Japanese population; the incidence of breast cancer among the female survivors is also increased (approximately three times).

21   X rays, by virtue of their energy, break molecules down into charged particles called ions. These highly reactive ions stimulate mitosis or destroy cells, depending on the dose and the tissue involved. How these effects are produced, and what factors trigger normal cells to divide and retain these proliferative properties, remain speculative, but mutations may be involved. We shall return to this later in the chapter.

Viruses and Cancer

22   As early as 1910 Peyton Rous found evidence that a fibrous connective-tissue tumor (sarcoma) in the breast muscle of chickens was due to the presence of a virus (Rous sarcoma virus, or RSV), but this was lightly dismissed as a peculiarity of chickens. Later, the evidence made such criticism less valid. In 1932 Rous, Beard, and Shope found that a nonmalignant skin cancer in wild rabbits was caused by a virus (Shope papilloma virus);[3] when the purified virus was transferred to other rabbits, it metastasized and eventually killed the animal. Today it is well recognized that viruses are responsible for a great many cancers. (In fact, Rous was awarded the 1966 Nobel Prize in medicine for his 1910 work on RSV.)

23   At the present time uncertainty

[3]Perhaps the best known of all human cancer that is viral in origin is the nonmalignant skin tumor known as the common wart. Electronmicroscopy reveals the presence of viruses in wart tissues; isolation of these viral particles and introduction into a susceptible host produce warts. (Handling toads has nothing to do with the transmission of warts.)

exists about whether viral invaders or viral residents already present within human cells are the causative agents of human cancers. The principal difficulty is this: the mere presence of viral particles in cancer cells does not necessarily *prove* viruses to be the cause of the condition. For example, it is conceivable that the viruses are harmless cellular occupants, and it is quite by chance that they occur within these cells, or it could be that viruses invade cells after the cells have been transformed into cancer cells and so have not contributed to the transformation process itself. A convincing demonstration that a virus does induce cancer is required, and certain criteria (called **Koch's postulates**) must be satisfied before we can say that proof positive has been obtained:

1. The virus must be isolated from the cancer.
2. The virus must be inoculated into a healthy animal and produce the disease.
3. The same virus must be reisolated from this experimentally induced cancer.

24   It is obvious that to apply such methods to the direct study of human cancers is almost impossible, and therefore other techniques have been employed. The transmission of human cancers to animals (other than humans) and to human cells grown outside the body in tissue-culture systems has provided a great deal of information on the nature of the relationship between viruses and human cancers, but the results are still far from conclusive (Figure 3–5). Presently, it is suspected that viruses may be involved in human cancers such as Burkitt's lymphoma (a tumor that destroys the jaw), breast cancer, leukemia, and Hodg-

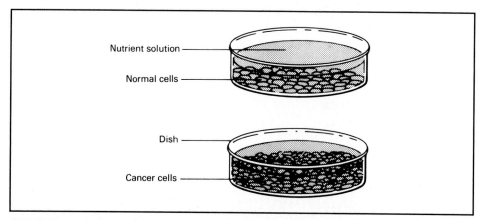

Nutrient solution

Normal cells

Dish

Cancer cells

FIGURE 3–5. Patterns of growth of normal and cancerous skin cells in tissue culture. In the lower dish the cancer cells are shown piled up.

kin's disease (a cancer of the spleen and lymph nodes). However, the assumption held by some that all cancers are caused by viruses, and that carcinogens such as chemicals and irradiations are effective because they activate the virus, is presently without foundation.

25 One of the problems involved in investigating virally induced cancers is that the behavior of viruses may depend on the host or the particular tissue that is invaded; in one tissue a virus may have no ill effects (it is simply a passenger virus), in another it may cause lethal effects, and in still others it may induce malignancy. To illustrate this let us look at a particular case.

26 In the early 1950s, Sarah E. Stewart and Bernice E. Eddy isolated a virus that caused salivary-gland tumors in mice. When reisolated and grown in tissue culture, the viruses multiplied, and upon reinjection into newborn mice, the viruses produced 20 different kinds of cancers in addition to the one found originally only in the salivary gland. This broad-spectrum virus was named **polyoma virus.** Other experiments using tissue cultures showed that, on occa-

sion, polyoma virus not only induced cells to become cancerous but resulted in cell death. What is responsible for these many faces of the polyoma virus?

27 The explanation may in part relate to the protein coat that surrounds the virus. The viral protein coat readily provokes an **immune response** by the host (that is, specific proteins called **antibodies** develop in the blood of the host upon contact with foreign proteins and the antibodies neutralize or inactivate the virus); when viruses are contracted in small quantities, the animal builds an immunity to the virus. In nature, polyoma virus is spread among mice in the saliva and in the feces, and the young gradually build an immunity to it.[4] Antibodies are also passed to the offspring via the mother's milk. This acquired immunity probably accounts for the low incidence of spontaneous tumors in mice. Experimentally, massive quantities of virus can be produced in tissue cultures, and then these can be injected into highly susceptible animals. In young

[4]Laboratory experimenters working with polyoma virus also build antibodies to it.

animals death often results because the defense system is unable to cope with the virus, but in older, more resistant animals the same virus may allow the host cells to live and cause them to proliferate; in this latter case, malignant cancers are produced.

28   How does the polyoma virus cause cancer? Electron microscopy shows the polyoma virus to be a round particle with a diameter of 2.7 Å, made up of a protein coat surrounding a core of DNA. When polyoma viruses enter a susceptible cell, the cell has two possible fates: (1) death, as a consequence of virus production, or (2) transformation into a cancer cell without the formation of new viruses. In both cases, viral particles are taken up by the host cell into small sacs, these sacs accumulate around the host-cell nucleus, some of the viruses lose their protein coats, and the naked viral DNA enters the nucleus. In the lethal infection, within 48 hours the host-cell nucleus becomes filled with viral particles; the progeny of the infecting viruses eventually fill the host cell and cause it to burst, and the released viral particles can begin a new round of infection. However, on rare occasions the polyoma virus can create a cancerous condition in the host cell. Viral particles are not seen in the transformed cell; rather, the naked viral DNA is inserted into the DNA of the host-cell chromosomes. These viral genes usurp and corrupt the host cell, making it act in a malignant way. How the viral DNA usurps the prerogatives of the host cell is still incompletely understood but some information is at hand.

29   Polyoma viral DNA carries about six to eight genes (it has 5,000 nucleotide base pairs); these genes are actively responsible for the production of a cancer cell. One of the viral genes probably codes for a protein that is a regulator (a promoter or repressor substance), and this turns on or off specific genes of the host cell or virus. . . . For example, the viral genes that code for viral coat protein are silent, or off, since once a cell is transformed, viruses with protein coats are never formed. On the other hand, the virus does turn on the cellular enzymes involved in DNA synthesis, presumably at the transcription level, thus causing both host-cell and viral genes to be duplicated and the cell to divide. In addition, viral genes direct the production of a specific coat on the host cell; this change in the host-cell surface may be responsible for the altered relations of the cancer cell with its neighbors.

30   Why do viruses induce cancer? The induction of cancer by some viruses may be a by-product of viral functions that have developed for their own multiplication. Because the virus is small, it cannot contain much genetic information and must therefore exploit the synthetic machinery of the cell to achieve its own replication. The viral activities induce cancer because they are similar to the activities and mechanisms by which cells regulate their own replication. In other words, viruses enter cells in order to reproduce their kind. To do this, they must turn on the DNA-replicating machinery of the host cell and redirect it to make viral materials. A side effect of continued DNA replication is likely to be continued cell division and proliferation—cancer.

—From *Biology: A Human Approach,* Third Edition, by Irwin W. Sherman and Vilia G. Sherman. Oxford University Press, 1979.

Postreading

TRUE OR FALSE

Directions: *Decide if each of the following statements is true (T) or false (F) based on the selection.*

_____ **1.** Cancer kills more people than any other disease.

_____ **2.** A cancer, or tumor, is composed of cells that grow and multiply autonomously.

_____ **3.** Malignant tumors at one time were benign.

_____ **4.** Benign tumors metastasize when they spread to other major organs.

_____ **5.** Carcinogens may be chemical, physical, or hormonal.

_____ **6.** Lung cancer is responsible for more than 75 percent of human cancers.

_____ **7.** All cancers are caused by viruses.

_____ **8.** Ultraviolet light is believed to be responsible for many skin cancers.

_____ **9.** Most experiments involving cancer studies use animals as opposed to human subjects.

_____**10.** Polyoma virus has been found to cause cancer.

_____**11.** Birth control pills cause breast cancer.

_____**12.** Most cancer is hereditary.

READING WORKSHEET

Directions: *After you have completed the true-or-false exercise, answer the following questions. You may refer to the selection, if necessary.*

1. One way that an author ensures comprehension is to repeat key words or to use synonyms of key words. How many times is the word *cancer* used in paragraph 1? _____

2. Locate *such events* in paragraph 2. What events are being referred to? _____

Describe how "some restraining influence" controls cellular growth.

_____

_____

3. Locate the last sentence in paragraph 3. A semicolon (;) is used to divide the sentence into two parts. The author could have connected these sentences with
   a. therefore.
   b. instead.
   c. on the other hand.

4. Read paragraph 4. What is being contrasted? _____

Who holds these different viewpoints? _____

5. What is the purpose of the last sentence in paragraph 1? _____

_____

in paragraph 4? _____

6. Locate the sentence in paragraph 6 beginning "The malignant invasive tumor . . . " Notice the use of a semicolon (;) again. What does this semicolon mean?
   a. in addition
   b. on the other hand
   c. after this

7. Read the second sentence in paragraph 7. What does this semicolon (;) mean?
   a. in other words
   b. so
   c. however

8. The author uses an analogy (a comparison of one idea or situation to another) to describe cancer. What does the author compare cancer to? _____

What is the Greek meaning of *cancer*? _____

9. There is a cause–effect relationship in paragraph 9. The result is signaled by *As a result*. Locate this sentence. What is the cause?

   _____

10. How many carcinogenic dietary agents are discussed? _____

    What are they? _____

    _____

11. Locate the sentence beginning "Long-term application . . . " in paragraph 12. The semicolon (;) in this sentence could be substituted with
    a. in other words.
    b. furthermore.
    c. because of this.

12. The author says that the amount of tar falling on Manhattan is "a small fraction of the 176 tons of solids that rain down on the inhabitants each month." Why does the author emphasize that the tar is only a small fraction? _____

13. There are cause–effect relationships expressed in paragraph 13. The result is a higher frequency of lung cancer. What is the cause?

    _____. What is the cause of

    atmospheric pollution? _____

14. Read the final sentence in paragraphs 11 and 12 and the final two sentences in paragraph 14. What can be said about the author's

    supporting information? _____

    What kind of evidence does the author use to support the claims

    in these paragraphs? _____

    What is the major weakness with animal experiments? _____

    _____

15. The author discusses the information given in Figure 3–3 in paragraph 15, stating that the greater increase in the incidence of lung cancer among men than women is due to "social habits." Look at

the graphs in Figure 3–3. Using the information given, describe the pattern of these habits. _____

_____

_____

16. What information was revealed in the study of the incidence of lung cancer in England?

    a. _____

    b. _____

    c. _____

17. What is the "warning" being referred to in paragraph 16? _____

_____

18. We read that "environmental agents are responsible for 75 percent of human cancers" (paragraph 18). Why do you think that environmental carcinogens are discussed first? _____

19. Locate the phrase, *but certain factors suggest that this may indeed be the case*. What does *this* refer to? _____

_____

20. What five factors contribute to the frequency of skin cancer?

    a. _____

    b. _____

    c. _____

    d. _____

    e. _____

21. Statistics are often used as strong support. In the section titled "X-radiation," three different statistics are used to support the claim that x-rays "are much more effective in producing cancer."

    a. "More effective" than what? _____

b. What statistics are reported? _____

    1. _____

    2. _____

    3. _____

22. Read the final sentence in paragraph 21. What will be returned to

later? _____

23. Why is *prove* italicized in paragraph 23? _____

24. At the end of paragraph 23 are three numbered sentences. Why

are they numbered? _____

What is the significance of these sentences? _____

_____

INFERENCE AND RESTATEMENT

Directions: *Decide whether each of the following is a restatement (R), an infer-*
ence (I), or a false statement (F) according to the selection. If the sentence is a
restatement, locate the original in the selection and give the paragraph number
where it is found.

_____ **1.** Even though they are considered harmless, benign tumors
should be removed because it is possible for them to become
malignant.

_____ **2.** People who work around carcinogenic agents have an increased
risk of developing cancer.

_____ **3.** When the population of an area is very dense, more pollutants
are introduced into the atmosphere, which may be responsible
for the increased levels of cancer in those areas.

_____ **4.** Human beings live longer than laboratory animals and are
exposed to carcinogens for a longer period of time. This increases their risk for developing cancer.

_____ **5.** It is possible that the layer of protein covering the cancer-producing polyoma virus may stimulate the immune system to develop antibodies against the virus.

_____ 6. Cigarette smoking causes cancer.

_____ 7. Cancer cells continue to multiply even after it is no longer necessary for them to do so.

_____ 8. Most cancer is caused by carcinogens introduced into the environment by humans.

_____ 9. The incidence of cancers of certain organs is higher in some geographic areas than in others.

_____10. Scientists are reasonably certain that viruses cause certain types of cancer.

OUTLINING

Directions: *Outlines are often written in two forms, those using complete sentences and those using phrases—most often noun or verb phrases. If you are writing down the most important ideas from a reading, it often is helpful to first write the outline using phrases. Then, as a good review, rewrite the outline using complete sentences.*

Below is information that will help you write an outline for the second part of the selection, "Carcinogens: Cancer-Causing Agents." As you reread this section, answer the questions below.

1. There are _____ main sections to this chapter. What are they?

    I. _____

    II. _____

2. We will review part of section II. Read the first paragraph in this section (paragraph 8). This section is broken down into _____ subsections:

    II. _____

        A. _____

        B. _____

        C. _____

3. How many parts are there to subsection A above? _____
What are they?

II. _____

    A. _____

        1. _____

        2. _____

        3. _____

        4. _____

        5. _____

4. What are the parts of subsection B above?

    B. _____

        1. _____

        2. _____

5. We now have an outline of the main ideas. In order to add detail
and examples to this section, we must expand our outline. Below
is an incomplete outline of part II-A, "Chemical Carcinogens." As
you reread this section, complete the outline.

II. _____

    A. Chemical

        1. _____

            a) _____ cancer found in chimney sweeps

                (1) Cause: _____

                (2) Chemical-causing agent: _____

        2. Dietary

            a) _____ found in _____

            b) _____ and _____

                (1) Bladder cancer in _____

            c) Diethylstilbestrol

                (1) _____ cancer

d) Chewing mixtures of _____, _____,

_____

(1) Cancers _____

(2) Countries used in:

(a) _____

(b) _____

3. _____

a) Female hormone: _____

(1) Long-term application = _____ in labora-

tory animals

(2) _____

(a) Higher incidence of:

(1) _____

(2) Uterine cancer

4. Atmospheric pollution

a) Cause: incompletely burned _____

(1) _____

(2) _____

(3) _____

(4) _____

b) Results

(1) _____

(2) _____

(3) _____

c) Example

(1) Where: _____

(2) What: _____ pounds of _____

each _____

(3) Cancer-causing agent: _____

(4) Result: _____

If you would like, you may outline the final section of this unit, "Smoking and Lung Cancer," in the same manner as we have done here. This section contains evidence supporting the relationship between cigarette smoking and lung cancer. As you outline, remember to note all the important evidence.

VOCABULARY FROM CONTEXT

You often will find that the author of a selection defines or describes key or new words immediately after, and sometimes before, the word is presented.

Example: Look at paragraph 1. Locate *ubiquitous killer*. Look at the sentence that follows. Try to guess what "ubiquitous killer" might be:

_____

What are some words from the reading that describe this phrase?

_____

Directions: *Using your own knowledge and information from the text, answer the following questions. Refer to the selection while you work. Don't be afraid to guess.*

1. Locate *morbidity statistics* in paragraph 1. Now look at the sentences that follow. What do you think morbidity statistics are? _____

   _____

2. Cancer is called *indiscriminate* (paragraph 1). Look at the list of people affected by cancer. Guess the meaning of *indiscriminate*.

   _____

   How does the author signal that the definition will be given after the term is used? _____

3. Locate *proliferation* in paragraph 2. The meaning of this word is described previously. What does proliferation mean? _____

   _____

4. How does the author help the reader define *neoplastic*? _____

   _____

From what language is the word derived? _____

How is this definition signaled? _____

5. Locate the footnote signaled by ¹. What is another term for *multip-lication* used in this footnote? _____

_____

6. What does *autonomous growth* (paragraph 4) mean? _____

How is this definition signaled? _____

SUMMARY

Directions: Fill in the blanks so that the following summary is logical, grammatically correct, and accurate according to the selection.

Cancer is the _____ leading cause of _____ in the United States following death from _____ disease. _____ is a condition that exists when cells begin uncontrolled _____. The body's immune system usually _____ to this uncontrolled _____ by trying to surround the abnormal _____ to keep them from invading _____ cells. If this effect _____, the cancer becomes _____ and may invade other parts of the body.

Although there are many _____ regarding the causes of cancer, researchers _____ that most cancer is caused by substances that occur in the environment. Some of these occur _____ but most have been introduced by _____. _____ believe that approximately _____ of all cancers are caused by environmental _____ and therefore are _____ preventable. _____ and _____ cancer are two examples of cancers which may be caused by the _____ of the victims themselves. As research progresses, the scientific community _____ to isolate the causes of this _____ and then

to find a _____.

ESSAY QUESTIONS

Directions: *In one to three paragraphs, answer the following questions using information from the selection to support your ideas.*

1. Describe the formation and behavior of cancerous cells.

2. Discuss the difference between a benign tumor and a malignant one. What happens when a benign tumor becomes malignant?

3. Discuss what changes a person could make in his or her personal habits that might reduce the risk of cancer.

RELATED READING

Human Mammary Tumors

Breast cancer is the most common type of cancer in women in the United States; there are 65,000 new cases each year and 25,000 deaths annually. In human breast cancer the earliest symptom is a lump in the breast; most commonly these are nonmalignant, or benign, tumors. Breast cancer risk increases with age, and the tumor seldom occurs in young women. As the cancer develops, it tends to spread to the lymphatics and then to other parts of the body; it is at this stage that the cancer is dangerous. Detection of cancer in the early stages is simple and effective. By self-examination of the breast more than 90 percent of breast cancers are discovered.

There is a tendency for breast cancer to occur more frequently in certain females, and this makes it likely that a genetic predisposition for it may exist (the genetic factor, if it exists, does not appear to be strong). Human breast cancers show hormone dependency. As early as 1896 G. Beatson, a British physician, found that surgical removal of the ovaries in patients with breast cancer caused a remission of the tumor. However, since breast cancer occurs more frequently among women who have never married and those who have not had children, the mechanism of hormonal action in human breast cancer remains an enigma. In mice, tumors of the mammary gland are also influenced by hormonal factors, but it has been conclusively shown that mammary tumors in mice are caused by a virus that was passed on in their mothers' milk. Although it seems to be different from the situation in the mouse, it may be that some human breast cancers are also viral in origin.

Treatment for breast cancer is ordinarily by surgery, but sometimes radiation and hormone therapy are employed. Cancer of the breast also occurs in men (the frequency is 1 case of male breast cancer for 100 cases of female breast cancer). The most common treatment for male breast cancer is, likewise, surgical removal.

In summary we can say that we know little about the events that initiate human breast cancer, but we do know that hormones play an im-portant role in the development and growth of mammary tumors. It is conceivable that the effect of hormones on the breast tissue produces an environment conducive to tumor formation; it is also possible that a combination of genetic and hormonal factors alone can induce tumor formation. Which, if any, of these is the causal mechanism remains uncertain at present.

—From *Biology: A Human Approach,* Third Edition, by Irwin W. Sherman and Vilia G. Sherman. Copyright © 1975, 1979, 1983 by Oxford University Press, Inc. Reprinted by permission.

DISCUSSION

Directions: Read the following questions. Be prepared to discuss them.

1. What is breast cancer?

2. What are its symptoms?

3. At what stage is the cancer dangerous?

4. How is this type of cancer treated?

5. What can be said about the causes of breast cancer?

6. What might cause breast cancer?

Trauma 4

RELATED READING

NEW TRAUMA CENTER SAVES LIVES

A young man lies uncon-scious after being stabbed in the heart. A passer-by notices him and calls for help. Paramedics reach the scene at 1:30 P.M.

Severly injured victims can now be treated in a newly constructed shock-trauma room at University Hospitals. This room con-tains equipment not usually found in hospital emergency rooms, such as facilities that enable a surgeon to perform on-the-spot surgery.

The shock-trauma room is located at the center of the hospital's emergency room, just steps from X-ray facil-ities, lab computers and blood banks. The room is divided into twin resuscitation bays by a wall with a win-dow. This allows visual com-munication between physi-cians when both areas are being used.

After evaluating the victim's condition, the paramedics place medical anti-shock trousers on the patient. These trousers grasp the skin to restore circulation. The para-medics also insert an endotracheal tube in his mouth to ensure an open airway for breathing. The victim arrives at the hospi-tal at 1:38 P.M.

Dr. Charles Cloutier and

Dr. Kenneth Kudsk, who officially opened the room August 31, are co-directors of the trauma center.

"This designated area has all the resources necessary for good trauma care," Cloutier said. The room, which is used six to ten times a week, "enables a physician to save critical minutes in the treatment of traumatized patients," he said.

Trauma is any serious injury or shock to the body. National statistics show that trauma is the leading killer of Americans between the ages of 1 and 44, taking the lives of more than 140,000 people a year.

Waiting for the stabbed victim at the hospital is a trauma team, who quickly transports the patient into the shock-trauma room. All vital signs, such as blood pressure and heart-rate, are taken. The victim does not respond.

Once the emergency room is notified that a severely injured patient will be arriv-ing, the hospital's operator alerts the trauma team by sending a signal. Each team member carries a beeper and can assemble at the room in one minute, Kudsk said.

University Hospitals'

trauma center has two trauma teams who work 24-hour rotating shifts. Survival of the seriously injured, Kudsk said, often depends "upon a well-trained team working together to minimize further injuries and decrease death rates."

Within minutes, the victim is prepared for surgery. The surgeon opens the chest and drains the blood from around the heart. After sewing up the wound, the surgeon pumps the heart and gives it an electroshock to in-itiate a heartbeat. The vic-tim's heart begins beating at 1:52 P.M.

The American College of Surgeons, a voluntary group of surgeons that evaluates trauma institutions, reviewed the hospital's trauma center and found that it met the criteria for a level-one trauma center. Level-one status is the highest rating a center can receive for its trauma care.

"Our center is the only level-one facility in the cen-tral or southeastern part of Ohio," Kudsk said.

Citing a study done in Phoenix, Arizona, Kudsk said, "When a severely in-jured patient went to a non-level-one institution, there was a 90 percent mortality rate. If taken to a level-one institution, only a 19 percent mortality rate existed." **After the victim's heartbeat is restored, he is taken upstairs to the main operating room. There he is thoroughly examined for other injuries. After leaving the operating room, the victim is taken to the intensive-care unit. The time is 2:10 P.M.**

—Courtesy of *The Lantern*.

DISCUSSION

Directions: Read the following questions. Be prepared to discuss them.

1. How do you think trauma centers are different from regular emergency rooms?

2. Do you think that trauma centers are more expensive than regular emergency rooms? Why or why not?

3. Why do you think the writer notes the time throughout the selection?

4. What is the purpose of the **boldface** in the selection?

5. Why do you think the author gives an account of an actual treatment at the trauma center?

6. Are trauma centers used in your country? If so, what do you know about their location and effectiveness? If not, what potential do you think there would be for trauma centers in your country?

Prereading

DISCUSSION

Directions: Read the following questions. Be prepared to discuss them.

1. Which of the following are examples of trauma?
   motorcycle injury
   headache
   knife wound
   drug overdose

2. Why do you think statistics are kept on the causes of death? Of what use could these statistics be to public officials? health officials? sociologists? future historians?

3. Have you ever witnessed a serious traffic accident? What care was given to the victim or victims at the scene of the accident?

4. What could be done to prevent serious injuries in offices and factories? on highways? in homes?

PREVIEW

Directions: Read the title and any subheadings of the selection. Also look at the illustrations and read any captions. Then, without reading the selection, answer the following questions.

1. Look at the caption on page 78; give the definitions of these terms:

   a. immediate death— _____

   _____

   b. early death— _____

   _____

   c. late death— _____

   _____

2. Judging from the information supplied by the graphs, what predictions can you make about the author's opinion of the importance of trauma as a major public health concern versus the attention paid to it by researchers and the health care professions? _____

_____

_____

3. Based on your answer to the preceding question, tell what you think is the author's purpose in writing this selection. _____

_____

4. What is the purpose of the space preceding certain paragraphs in the selection, for example, paragraphs 1 and 7? What do you suppose it signals? _____

_____

5. Skim paragraphs 1 through 6. What information do these paragraphs give? _____

_____

6. Skim paragraphs 9 through 19 and list the five trauma prevention programs that the author discusses.

   a. _____

   b. _____

   c. _____

   d. _____

   e. _____

READING

TRAUMA

Accidental and intentional injuries account for more years of life lost in the U.S. than cancer and heart disease. Among the prescribed remedies are improved preventive efforts, speedier surgery and further research.

DONALD D. TRUNKEY

1   Trauma is the medical term for a personal injury or wound. Including both accidental and intentional injuries, physical trauma is the principal cause of death among Americans between the ages of 1 and 38. In 1982 there were about 165,000 deaths from trauma in the U.S., and for each death there were at least two cases of permanent disability. Statistics compiled by the Department of Health and Human Services indicate that for Americans between the ages of 15 and 24 the combined death rate from motor-vehicle accidents, homicides and suicides has risen by 50 percent since 1976. Among young whites motor-vehicle accidents are the leading cause of death, accounting for about 40 percent, whereas among young blacks homicide is the leading cause of death, account-

ing for approximately the same percentage. In large cities black males have a 1-in-20 chance of being murdered before the age of 30. Increased urban violence has been a major contributor to the rise in the national homicide rate: from 8,464 in 1960 to more than 26,000 in 1982. Overall the death rate for American teenagers and young adults is 50 percent higher than it is for their contemporaries in other industrialized societies.

2   Because trauma primarily affects people at or near the beginning of their most productive work years, its cost measured in lost productivity from both death and disability is high: more than $63 million per day in lost wages from accidental trauma alone, according to a recent estimate by the National Safety Council. The total annual cost of accidental trauma, including lost wages, medical expenses and indirect work losses, comes to about $50 billion.

3   Trauma patients currently take up a total of about 19 million hospital days per year in the U.S., more than the number needed by all heart-disease patients and four times the number needed by all cancer patients. In the past decade the death rate from heart disease and stroke has fallen

by 22 and 32 percent respectively. In contrast the death rate from accidents has risen by about 1 percent per year since 1977. Trauma is clearly a major medical and social problem in the U.S. To a large extent, however, it is being neglected by physicians, hospital administrators, government officials and the general public.

4   Data from several parts of the country show that death from trauma has a trimodal distribution: when the death rate is plotted as a function of time after injury, three peaks appear in the resulting graph [*see illustration on page 78*]. The first peak, characterized as "immediate deaths," represents people who die very soon after an injury. Invariably these deaths are caused by lacerations of the brain stem, the spinal cord, the heart or one of the major blood vessels. Only a fraction of the patients in this category could in principle be saved, even under the most favorable medical conditions.

5   The second peak, characterized as "early deaths," represents people who die within the first few hours after an injury. These deaths are usually caused by major internal hemorrhages of the head, the respiratory system or the abdominal organs, or by multiple lesser injuries

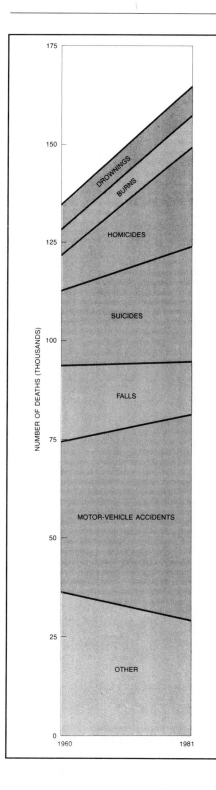

175

150

125

100 NUMBER OF DEATHS (THOUSANDS)

75

50

25

0

1960   1981

DROWNINGS

BURNS

HOMICIDES

SUICIDES

FALLS

MOTOR-VEHICLE ACCIDENTS

OTHER

Trends in mortality from trauma in the U.S. are plotted according to the cause of death in this graph, representing data gathered by the National Center for Health Statistics. The figures for 1960 are either actual totals for that year or averages for the period from 1952 through 1963; figures for 1981 are based on a 10 percent sample of that year's deaths.

resulting in severe blood loss. Almost all injuries of this type are considered treatable by currently available medical procedures. The interval between injury and definitive treatment, however, is critical to the probability of recovery.

6   The third peak, characterized as "late deaths," represents people who die days or weeks after an injury. In almost 80 percent of these cases the cause of death is either infection or multiple organ failure. Here time is less of a factor than the quality of medical care and the extent of medical knowledge. In what follows I shall discuss the pathology of each peak in somewhat greater detail, with particular reference to the prospects for reducing the rate of mortality and disability resulting from the associated set of medical conditions.

7   More than half of all trauma deaths are classified as immediate. The small number of patients in this category who could be saved are those in the few large cities where rapid transportation is available and special facilities called trauma centers are in operation. A trauma center is a hospital where the medical staff has made a commitment to provide 24-hour "in-house" coverage by surgeons, anesthesiologists and supporting staff to care for trauma patients. Recent medical records from two of these centers, one in Seattle and the

other in San Francisco, indicate that if there are signs of life at the scene of an accident or on the way to the hospital, 20 percent of the patients who are classified as "dead on arrival" can be resuscitated in the emergency room and will eventually leave the hospital without permanent neurological damage.

8   This remarkable rate of recovery will probably never be achieved in most suburban and rural settings, because of the longer time it usually takes there between

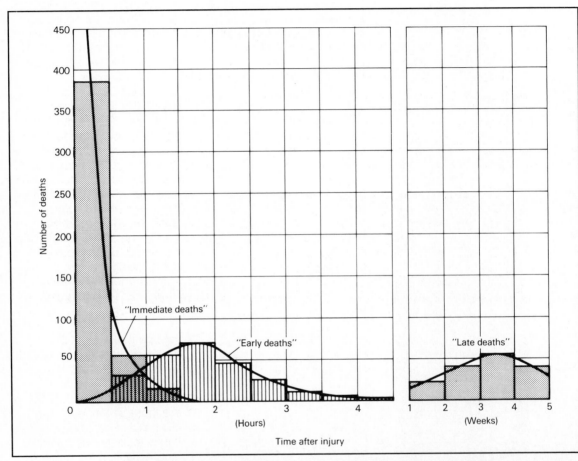

Trimodal distribution of trauma deaths is observed when the death rate for a large enough sample of such deaths is plotted as a function of time after injury. The first peak ("Immediate deaths") corresponds to people who die very soon after an injury; the deaths in this category are typically caused by lacerations of the brain, the brain stem, the upper spinal cord, the heart or one of the major blood vessels. The second peak ("Early deaths") corresponds to people who die within the first few hours after an injury; most of these deaths are attributable to major internal hemorrhages or to multiple lesser injuries resulting in severe blood loss. The third peak ("Late deaths") corresponds to people who die days or weeks after an injury; these deaths are usually due to infection or multiple organ failure. The graph is based on a sample of 862 trauma deaths recorded over a two-year period by the author's group at San Francisco General Hospital.

injury and definitive treatment. The only way to reduce the number of immediate deaths in these circumstances is through prevention. Perhaps as many as 40 percent of all deaths from trauma could be averted by the introduction of various prevention programs. Most of these programs involve controversial social issues, however, and so their chances of success are unpredictable. I shall cite here just a few of the more important trauma-prevention programs that have been proposed.

9   According to the Insurance Institute for Highway Safety, between 50 and 60 percent of the fatal motor-vehicle accidents in the U.S. are caused by drunk drivers. Efforts to reduce drunk driving by increasing the penalties for infractions have generally failed in the U.S., and similar programs in Europe have had only mixed results. For example, reports from a number of Scandinavian countries indicate that after mandatory jail sentences for drunk driving were imposed a significant reduction in fatal accidents was observed. In time, however, there was usually a reversion to the same mortality rate that had prevailed before the stronger measures were introduced. Rehabilitation programs for drunk drivers, introduced in several parts of the U.S., have also been found to be ineffective.

10   In spite of this generally negative record there is some evidence that the suspension or revocation of a driver's license after a drunk-driving conviction can have a significant effect on the subsequent rate of drunk-driving arrests in the affected population. Recently a "grass roots" group called Mothers Against Drunk Drivers (MADD)* was organized in California to promote such stronger measures to reduce the carnage caused by drunk drivers. The impact of this campaign, which is now spreading to other parts of the country, remains to be seen.

11   Another vexing social issue with a bearing on the current rate of trauma focuses on the mandatory use of safety devices such as automobile seat belts and motorcycle helmets. Legislation requiring the use of seat belts has been introduced in at least 20 countries. The results of these measures vary, depending on the degree of enforcement and compliance. So far the best record has been achieved in Australia, where after a law was passed requiring the use of seat belts there was a 27 percent decrease in the death rate from motor-vehicle accidents. Mandatory seat-belt legislation has not been popular in the U.S., however, in part because of the active resistance of groups opposed to such forms of Federal regulation.

* Now called Mothers Against Drunk Driving.

12   The situation is equally unsettled in the case of laws requiring the use of motorcycle helmets. Beginning in 1967 a Federal highway-safety standard required that all states enact and enforce motorcycle-helmet laws. In the next decade fatalities from motorcycle accidents decreased by 50 percent nationally. Then in 1976 Congress revoked the sanctions against states not in compliance with the Federal standard. Over the next three years 27 states repealed or weakened their motorcycle-helmet laws. The result so far has been a 40 percent increase in the death rate from motorcycle accidents in those states. A recent study sponsored by the National Highway Traffic Safety Administration concluded that "the use of a safety helmet is the single most critical factor in the prevention or reduction of head injury" from motorcycle accidents.

13   The burden placed on society by unhelmeted motorcyclists can be demonstrated. In one study of 71 motorcyclists admitted to Denver General Hospital it was found that only 38 percent were covered by commercial medical insurance or workman's compensation; most of the unpaid bills were borne by the taxpayers. Similarly, in a survey done at the Maryland Institute for Emergency Medical Services it was found that 40 percent of the 60 motorcyclists hos-

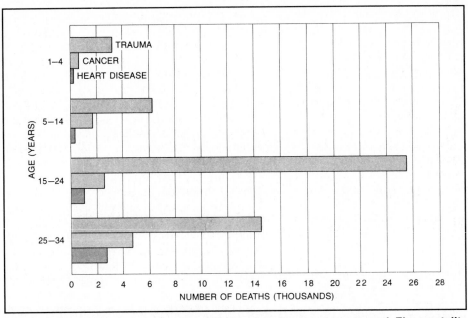

Three leading causes of death among young Americans are compared. The mortality figures, compiled by workers at the National Center for Health Statistics, are for 1977.

pitalized did not have insurance coverage.

14   Perhaps the most controversial trauma-prevention issue in the U.S. is that of handgun control. According to advocates of greater restrictions on the availability of handguns, more than 11,000 of the 26,000 murders recorded in the U.S. in 1982 were committed with such weapons. In addition, suicides and accidents involving handguns accounted for at least 10,000 deaths. Both figures are extraordinarily high, particularly in comparison with other industrialized societies, where handguns are controlled. There are at present some 60 million handguns in the U.S., and it can be argued that it would be difficult, if

not impossible, to eliminate them entirely, even if the political will to do so were to prevail in Congress. In the meantime other approaches to handgun control, such as the institution of mandatory jail sentences for the criminal use of a handgun, might help to reduce the death rate from gunshot wounds. Laws of this kind have been passed in several states, and the results, particularly in Michigan, seem to be quite positive.

15   Another controversial issue is that of the decriminalization of narcotic drugs. In the 15 years that I have worked as a surgeon at the University of California at San Francisco General Hospital Medical Center the number

of victims of penetrating trauma (primarily gunshot and stab wounds) has increased to approximately 40 percent of the total trauma caseload. Almost all of these injuries are related to drug trafficking. Most drug addicts must pay for their habit by illegal means, and violent crime is a common recourse. The decriminalization of drugs could help to solve at least this part of the drug problem.

16   Supporters of decriminalization argue further that the prevalence of drug abuse is not significantly dependent on the legal status of the drug in question. The experience of this country in the 1920's suggests that the consumption of alcohol was not reduced by prohibition;

indeed, it may even have been increased. There is no reason to believe drug abuse would be greatly affected one way or the other by decriminalization. What is certain is that many of the negative social effects accompanying drug abuse would be alleviated.

17   Finally, there is the problem of burn injuries, which in many respects is representative of the larger trauma-prevention problem. More than two million Americans per year suffer from burns of one kind or another, and of them some 70,000 are admitted to a hospital. Of the latter group 8,000 or so eventually die of their burn injuries. More than a third of these deaths are attributable to cigarette smoking. The average American cigarette contains additives in both the paper and the tobacco that cause the cigarette to burn for approximately 28 minutes. If these additives were omitted, the cigarette would burn out in less than four minutes. As it happens, most furniture, upholstery and mattresses made in the U.S. need more than four minutes' exposure to a burning cigarette for ignition. The problem and the solution are obvious. Omitting the incendiary additives from cigarettes would not change the taste of the cigarette smoke, but it would make smoking safer by reducing fire-related deaths, disabilities and property losses.

18   Of course, the cigarette manufacturers are not about to remove these additives voluntarily. That change undoubtedly calls for Federal legislation. Just as in the

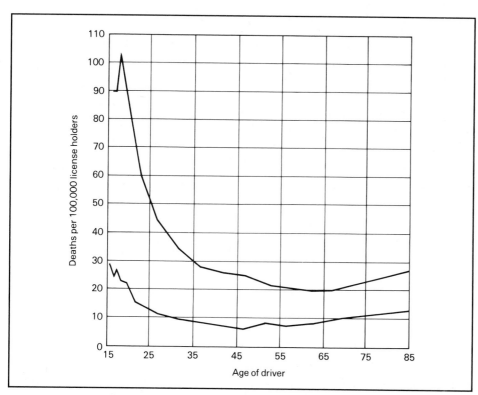

Young male drivers account for a disproportionately high percentage of deaths from motor-vehicle accidents, as is shown in this graph of the death rate for male drivers and female drivers. Curves, for 1978, are from the Insurance Institute for Highway Safety.

case of motor-vehicle accidents caused by drunk driving, fires caused by cigarette smoking bring death and disability to innocent people as well as to the individuals responsible for the accidents. Beyond the question of controlling cigarette additives, other burn prevention proposals call for measures to promote such practices as the manufacture of flame-resistant clothing, the installation of smoke alarms, the shortening of cords on appliances and the reduction of water-heater temperatures to prevent scalds of small children.

19   Although the preceding discussion is not a complete catalogue of trauma-prevention issues, it does indicate some of the problems such proposals face in the U.S. Clearly these issues are complex and impinge on long-established social customs. Nevertheless, prevention remains the only feasible way to reduce the toll of immediate deaths from trauma. It is not only the most effective way to save lives but also the cheapest: crisis intervention after the fact is always expensive. Ultimately prevention could also help to reduce the other two death peaks from trauma, topics I shall now address.

20   Roughly 30 percent of the deaths from trauma fall into the category of early deaths. This category can in turn be subdivided into two major pathological conditions:

neurological injuries and various kinds of hemorrhage. According to a recent nationwide survey of head and spinal-cord injuries, head injuries account for about .2 percent of all hospital admissions in the U.S. On this basis one can calculate that roughly 34,000 cases of traumatic intracranial bleeding are treated annually in the U.S.

21   The results of another recent study, done by a group at the Health Sciences Division of Virginia Commonwealth University, point to the need for prompt management of such head injuries. The Virginia group found that if surgical intervention for intracranial bleeding was delayed for more than four hours after an injury, the most probable outcome was death or permanent disability. If definitive surgical care was provided within four hours after an injury, however, the likelihood of a favorable outcome was significantly enhanced.

22   The need for prompt, definitive surgical intervention is also critical in the treatment of patients with injuries resulting in hemorrhage. For the sake of discussion hemorrhage can be divided into three grades: severe, moderate and minor. In cases of severe hemorrhage the rate of blood loss exceeds 150 milliliters per minute. In the first 10 minutes of severe hemorrhage the patient will lose at least 1,500 milliliters of blood, or roughly a third of his blood

volume. If this rate continues unchecked, the patient will lose more than half of his blood volume within 20 minutes of the injury. In such cases little can be done in the prehospital setting to control the hemorrhage. Prompt, definitive surgical care offers this patient his only chance of survival.

23   In cases of moderate hemorrhage the bleeding rate is between 30 and 150 milliliters per minute, and there will be a life-threatening blood loss within an hour of the injury. Rapid transport of the patient to a place where prompt surgical intervention is available is also the preferred treatment. Patients with minor hemorrhage (bleeding rates of less than 30 milliliters per minute) may have the "luxury" of an hour or more before surgical intervention is necessary. In addition intravenous lines started in the prehospital setting may keep up with the bleeding. In any case the main point remains that many early deaths from trauma could be prevented by rapid transport of the injured patient to a trauma center.

24   Are trauma patients in the U.S. receiving the kind of timely medical care these studies indicate they need? Several sources show that with the exception of a few communities having modern trauma centers the answer is no. For example, in 1960 investigators from the Surgeon General's office in Texas examined the deaths of 606 soldiers injured in

accidents and treated in community hospitals. They found that 96 of the patients would have survived if appropriate treatment had been administered in time, and an additional 103 patients might have been saved if they had been treated appropriately. Another study, done by workers at the University of Michigan in 1969, showed that 28 of 159 patients who died as a result of trauma were inadequately treated. Still another study, reported by a group at Johns Hopkins University in 1972, showed that a third of the deaths resulting from motor-vehicle accidents involving abdominal injuries in the Baltimore area could have been prevented by prompt surgical intervention.

25   I have been personally involved in several studies of this kind in the San Francisco Bay area. The first study, reported in 1974, compared the death records from the trauma center at San Francisco General Hospital with those from several community hospitals in the surrounding area. The results showed that patients with injuries from motor-vehicle accidents treated in a hospital without a trauma center had a significantly greater chance of dying than those treated in the one with a trauma center. A subsequent study compared deaths caused by motor-vehicle accidents in one part of California where there was no trauma center (Orange

County) with those in a part of the state that had a single designated trauma center (San Francisco). Again the outcome was significantly worse in the region without a trauma center.

26   The latter finding led to a follow-up study, initiated by physicians in the Orange County area. The data were reevaluated by an independent group of general surgeons, neurosurgeons and emergency-room physicians. Their report showed that non-neurological trauma care was inadequate in the hospitals without a designated trauma center. As a consequence five trauma centers were established in the Orange County area in 1980.

27   Another pertinent study was recently completed by the same group. It showed that the preventable-death category in Orange County dropped from 73 percent to 4 percent when patients were taken to a trauma center rather than to a conventional hospital. Furthermore, the group found that none of the patients in the study died as a result of bypassing a conventional hospital in order to get to a trauma center. This finding emphasizes the importance of regional trauma care. Numerous other studies in various parts of the country lend further support to the conclusion that injured patients taken to hospitals without a trauma center are at a marked disadvantage. On the average the incidence of

preventable deaths resulting from inadequate trauma care was found in these studies to vary between 30 and 40 percent.

28   Perhaps the most comprehensive study of this kind was done in 1980 by Daniel K. Lowe and his associates at the Oregon Health Sciences University. The study included 23 hospitals in a six-county region around Portland. The region has a total extent of 5,724 square miles and a population of 1,257,450, distributed over urban, suburban and rural areas. Originally 763 trauma patients were enrolled in the study; of these 104 had minor injuries and were excluded from further consideration. Of the 659 remaining patients there were 105 cases of inappropriate care, as determined by an independent trauma panel composed of general surgeons, neurosurgeons and emergency-room physicians. Of the 278 deaths registered 135 occurred in the hospital, and of these 34 were judged preventable by the panel. The latter group included 15 patients with brain injuries and 19 with various kinds of hemorrhage.

29   Of particular interest in the Portland results was the finding concerning the response time of the surgical consultants. In general the surgical consultants (there were 304 in all) took an average of 1.26 hours to get to the hospital after being called into the case. Neurological consultants re-

sponded somewhat more promptly: the average was .98 hour. The independent panel considered delayed response to be a significant factor in some of the cases of inadequate care. This finding draws attention to another problem: the popular misconception that any physician can treat a trauma patient adequately in a hospital emergency room. The emergency-room physician can start resuscitation, but a surgeon is almost always needed to provide definitive care. The sooner this care is provided, the better the outcome will be.

30   These findings all lead to one conclusion: There is a major shortfall in the delivery of trauma care in the U.S. The number of preventable deaths resulting from the existing system (or nonsystem) of trauma care is clearly unacceptable. What can be done to organize a better system of trauma care in the U.S.?

31   The concept of organized trauma care is not a new one; indeed, it can be traced back in military history to antiquity. The earliest mention of organized battlefield care is in the *Illiad*. According to Homer, Greek soldiers wounded in the fighting for Troy were carried off the battlefield and cared for in barracks (called *klisiai*) or on nearby ships. The *Illiad* contains references to 147 different wounds and implies a mortality rate of 77 percent.

32   The Romans also had considerable experience with emergency care for the injured; as early as 480 B.C. wounded soldiers were reportedly assigned to the care of patrician families. By the first century A.D. special hospitals (called *valetudinaria*) had been established along the borders of the Roman Empire to care for wounded legionaries. Archaeologists have identified at least 25 of these structures, which were quite sophisticated in design.

33   In the early 19th century Baron Dominique Jean Larrey, the chief surgeon in the army of Napoleon, made two improvements in the care of wounded soldiers that have persisted to modern times. The first was the *ambulance volante* ("flying hospital"), an innovation that sharply reduced the time it took to provide definitive care to the wounded. Before the advent of Larrey's horse-drawn ambulances injured soldiers often lay on the battlefield for periods of a day or more. Larrey's second innovation was to concentrate the casualties in one area and to operate on them as close to the front lines as possible.

34   During World War I the time lag between injury and surgery was still between 12 and 18 hours, and the overall mortality rate was 8.5 percent. The time lag was reduced in World War II to between 6 and 12 hours, and the mortality rate fell to 5.8 percent. Perhaps the most dramatic reduction in the time lag from injury to definitive surgical treatment came during the Korean conflict. A decision was made in the U.S. Army Medical Corps to bypass the battalion aid station and to take injured soldiers directly from the battlefield to a mobile army surgical hospital (M.A.S.H.). The average time lag between injury and definitive care during the Korean conflict was between two and four hours, and the mortality rate was 2.4 percent.

35   This tactic was further improved on during the U.S. involvement in Vietnam, where casualties were taken directly from the battlefield to the corps surgical hospital. According to one study, the average time lag between injury and definitive surgical care was reduced to 65 minutes, and the mortality rate fell to 1.7 percent. This military experience, one might think, should have served as an incentive and a model for the improvement of civilian trauma-care systems. With the exception of a few isolated instances, however, that has not happened.

36   One example of excellent regional trauma care can be found in West Germany. During the late 1960's West German health officials observed the U.S. methods of providing battlefield care in Vietnam. In 1970 the decision was made to apply these procedures throughout most of West Germany, establishing trauma centers along the main autobahns.

Integral to the trauma-center concept in West Germany is rapid prehospital transport, which primarily entails the use of helicopters but also includes ground vehicles. There are now 32 air-rescue 37 stations in the country with a standard mission radius of 50 kilometers. It is estimated that 90 percent of the population are within 15 minutes of a trauma center.

More important than the prehospital system is the system of integrated trauma care within the hospitals. West German hospitals have been classified according to their ability to provide trauma care. Futhermore, there is

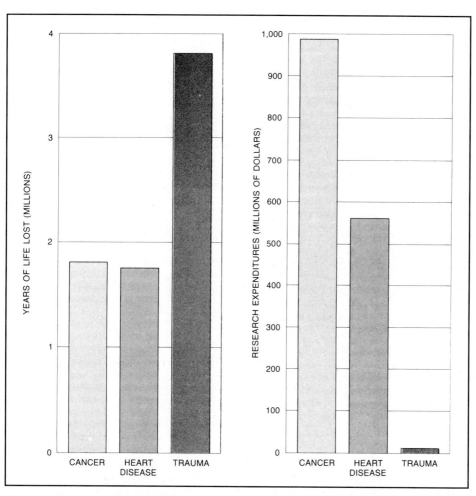

Mismatch between the cost of trauma, in terms of the number of years of life lost, and the national effort to solve the trauma problem, in terms of dollars spent on research, is particulary striking in the context of a comparison with the corresponding figures for cancer and heart disease. The bars in the left-hand chart are based on an estimate published in the Surgeon General's report for 1975. The bars in the right-hand chart are based on 1982 figures from the National Institutes of Health; they refer only to research funds spent under the auspices of the National Cancer Institute, the National Heart, Lung, and Blood Institute and (in the case of trauma research) the National Institute of General Medical Sciences.

an in-house team of surgeons in every designated trauma center on a 24-hour basis. The teams include not only surgical residents but also a chief surgeon. The other important members of the trauma team are a neurosurgeon and an anesthesiologist. The chief trauma surgeon also cares for the patient in the post-operative period, including the time spent in the intensive-care unit. Overall the quality of surgical care is excellent.

38   The West German system also has a strong rehabilitation program, the primary goal of which is to get the accident victim back to gainful employment as soon as possible. I do not mean to imply that the system there is perfect. Some of the trauma centers are not as strong as they should be, but in general the system is an excellent model for the U.S.

39   As a consequence of this regionalized system the mortality rate from motor-vehicle accidents in West Germany has dropped from 16,000 per year in 1970 to 12,000 per year at present, a reduction of 25 percent. It is probably more than a coincidence that the magnitude of this reduction is remarkably close to the preventable-death estimate made in most American studies (between 30 and 40 percent). By applying simple arithmetic and assuming that the 4,000 additional German patients who now survive each year

return to work, a rough estimate of the financial benefit to that society can be made. If one assumes that each survivor over the past 10 years now earns the equivalent of $10,000 per year and pays $2,500 in taxes, the gross national product of West Germany would be increased by $220 million per year and tax revenues would rise by $55 million. The value of a trauma center, therefore, lies not only in a reduction in deaths and disabilities but also in a positive financial contribution to society. If the U.S. were to introduce a similar system and could achieve the same reduction in mortality, then over the first 10 years this country's G.N.P. could be increased by more than $2 billion and the additional taxes paid would amount to more than $550 million.

40   The final category in this discussion, late deaths, accounts for approximately a fifth of all trauma deaths. Of these deaths 80 percent are attributable to infection and multiple organ failure. The two conditions seem to be casually related. The common risk factors that have been identified so far include shock, head injury, peritoneal contamination and malnutrition, all of which can lead to infections late in the course of a patient's injury. This development may in turn be related to the failure of the patient's immune system, but the exact causes have not been elucidated. Once

infection is obvious the patient often develops progressive organ failure. The resulting mortality rate is high and is directly related to the number of organ systems involved.

41   The answer to the question of why the trauma patient is at risk for infection and multiple organ failure can only come from further research. Even this solution, however, is not without difficulties. At present the U.S. spends very little of its research funds on trauma. National priorities are clearly directed to cancer and heart disease, even though trauma accounts for more years of life lost than cancer and heart disease combined. One solution would be to establish a National Institute of Trauma, on the model of the National Cancer Institute or the National Heart, Lung, and Blood Institute. Such an institute could serve many purposes. It could focus on trauma both as a medical issue and as a social one. It could approach trauma in such a way as to place equal emphasis on prevention, health-care delivery and research aimed toward the solution of the late-deaths problem. It could also serve as a focus for innovative ideas in research funding. For example, since drunk driving is a major contributor to the national trauma rate, perhaps it would be feasible to devote part of the tax on alcoholic beverages to help support trauma research.

42   Finally, there is the prob-

lem of rehabilitation. One of the most pronounced deficiencies in trauma care in the U.S. is the lack of an integrated rehabilitation system. Most disabling injuries are caused by neurological and orthopedic injuries. With the exception of some excellent rehabilitation centers for spinal-cord injuries the U.S. has not placed enough emphasis on returning the injured patient to work. This approach should involve not only physical rehabilitation but also job retraining and treatment of the emotional trauma that often accompanies physical trauma. In order to have an effective rehabilitation system the nation must also address some of the existing worker's compensation laws and disability-reimbursement programs. For example, an employed person or union member currently takes five times as much disability time as a person who is self-employed. Any proposed rehabilitation system must address the disincentives that affect the decision to return to work.

43   In summary, trauma is a seriously neglected public-health problem in the U.S. Each of the three peaks in the trimodal distribution of trauma deaths has its own set of associated problems. If the U.S. is to achieve a significant reduction in the rate of mortality and disability from trauma, each of these issues must be addressed vigorously. The solutions will not be easy, and they will inevitably engage some controversial social issues. It is my contention, however, that the U.S. can no longer afford the present rate of preventable death and disability resulting from trauma. The search for solutions to the trauma problem must become a national priority.

—From "Trauma," Donald D. Trunkey. *Scientific American*, 1983.

Postreading

TRUE OR FALSE

Directions: Decide if each of the following statements is true (T) or false (F) based on the selection.

_____ **1.** The leading cause of death among young Americans is cancer, followed closely by trauma.

_____ **2.** Work time lost because of trauma costs about $50 billion dollars per year.

_____ **3.** When mandatory jail sentences were given to drunk drivers in Scandinavia, there was a permanent decrease in the number of fatal traffic accidents.

_____ **4.** Motorcycle-helmet laws passed in 1967 were effective in reducing fatal motorcycle injuries by 50 percent.

_____ **5.** According to the author, trauma victims in the United States currently receive inadequate care.

_____ **6.** The U. S. Army developed high-quality trauma care during the American Civil War.

_____ **7.** West Germany modeled its trauma-care system after the one currently in use in the United States.

_____ **8.** Most of the people in West Germany live very near a trauma center.

_____ **9.** A trauma center has a special surgery team available twenty-four hours a day.

_____**10.** According to the selection, the number of preventable trauma deaths could be significantly reduced with the establishment of more trauma centers.

READING WORKSHEET

Directions: After you have completed the true-or-false exercise, answer the following questions. You may refer to the selection if necessary.

1. In writing a persuasive essay, an author often uses two separate

88

thesis statements—an "Is" thesis (which controls the development of the essay) and an "Ought" thesis. What do you think is the purpose of each type of thesis statement?

a. Is— _____

_____

_____

b. Ought— _____

_____

_____

2. Keeping in mind what you know about the organization of an essay, where would you expect to find the thesis statement?

_____

_____

3. Locate and copy the "Is" thesis of this selection.

_____

_____

4. Which is the best paraphrase of the following sentence from paragraph 1: "Among young whites motor-vehicle accidents are the leading cause of death, accounting for about 40 percent, whereas among young blacks homicide is the leading cause of death, accounting for approximately the same percentage."
  a. White people have a 40 percent chance of dying in a car accident, while blacks have the same chance of being murdered.
  b. Forty percent of young white people who die are victims of auto accidents, while 40 percent of young black people who die are murdered.
  c. Out of 100 people who die, 40 will be whites involved in motor-vehicle accidents and 40 will be blacks who are murdered.

5. In the last sentence in paragraph 1, what is meant by the phrase *their contemporaries*? _____

6. Thinking about what you know about the prefix *tri- (tricycle, triangle),* guess the meaning of the word *trimodal* in paragraph 4. (Hint: If you can't guess from the prefix itself, read the entire sentence again.)

_____

7. Looking at the sentence in paragraph 4 that begins "Only a fraction of the patients in this category could in principle be saved," what does *in principle* mean? How would the meaning be changed if the phrase were *in practice*? _____

_____

8. Which of the following is the best paraphrase of the following sentence from paragraph 5: "The interval between injury and definitive treatment, however, is critical to the probability of recovery."
   a. The period between the time of the injury and the time the definition of treatment begins is important to the best chance of recovery.
   b. The time of the injury defines the treatment and the probability of recovery.
   c. The time that goes by before specific treatment is received is a great factor in the chance of recovery.

9. Look at the graph on page 77. What is plotted against the number of deaths? _____ For what years? _____ Which causes of death increased over the period shown? _____ Which decreased? _____ Which remained the same? _____ What is the source of the data? _____

10. In paragraph 10, the author refers to Mothers Against Drunk Driving as a "grass roots" organization. What image does this term recall? Suggest a synonym. _____

_____

11. Why do you think rehabilitation programs and increased penalties generally have failed to reduce drunk driving?

_____

_____

12. What is the "vexing social issue" that the author introduces in paragraph 11? Why does he consider it vexing? _____

_____

13. What facts does the author give to support his statement that "the burden placed on society by unhelmeted motorcyclists can be demonstrated" (paragraph 13)? _____

_____

14. According to the graph on page 81, which of the following statements is *not* correct?
a. The greatest number of deaths from motor-vehicle accidents among young men occurs roughly at age 18.
b. A decrease in motor-vehicle accidents occurs among adults over 65.
c. More than three times the number of men compared to women, at the age of 25, are killed in motor-vehicle accidents.

15. Why do you think that handgun control is "perhaps the most controversial trauma-prevention issue in the U.S." (paragraph 14)?

_____

16. What benefit does the author give for the decriminalization of drugs? _____

_____

17. Choose the best restatement of the first sentence in paragraph 16.
a. People who want to make drugs legal say that drug abuse does not really depend on whether a drug is legal or not.
b. People who support making drugs legal argue about the question of the status of drug abuse.
c. Criminals who support significant drug abuse believe that legal status is in question.

18. How is the problem of burn injuries representative of the larger trauma-prevention problem? _____

_____

_____

19. Look at the graph on page 80. What does this graph show?

_____

What age groups are plotted against the number of deaths?

_____

What is the leading cause of death for children between the ages of 5 and 14? _____ Which causes of death increased over the periods shown? _____

Which decreased? _____

Which remained the same? _____

What is the source of the data? _____

20. Does the author believe trauma patients in the United States receive timely and appropriate care? _____

What information is used to support his conclusion? _____

_____

21. In paragraphs 31 through 35 the author discusses the history of trauma care from the time of the early Greeks through the Vietnam War. What point do you feel that he is trying to make with this discussion?

_____

_____

_____

22. Choose the best paraphrase of the following sentence from paragraph 36: "Integral to the trauma-center concept in West Germany is rapid prehospital transport, which primarily entails the use of helicopters but also includes ground vehicles."
   a. The speedy transportation of patients before they reach the hospital (mainly using helicopters but also ground vehicles) is critical to the concept of the trauma center in West Germany.
   b. The trauma center integrates helicopters and ground vehicles in the concept of prehospital transportation, which is crucial in West Germany.
   c. The primary use of helicopters and ground vehicles in West

Germany is crucial to the trauma center concept integrated with prehospital transportation.

23. Briefly state a conclusion that can be drawn from a comparison of the bar graphs on page 85. _____

_____

_____

24. What solutions does the author suggest to correct the problem of lack of research (and funding thereof) concerning trauma?

_____

_____

_____

25. With what paragraph does the conclusion of the selection begin? _____ What phrase signals this? _____

INFERENCE AND RESTATEMENT

Directions: *Decide whether each of the following is a restatement (R), an inference (I), or a false statement (F) according to the selection. If the sentence is a restatment, locate the original in the selection and give the number of the paragraph where it is found.*

_____ **1.** Only 10 percent of West Germany's population lives more than 15 minutes from a trauma center.

_____ **2.** Trauma centers should be established in the United States because the people whose lives are saved can make significant economic contributions to the society in the form of taxes.

_____ **3.** West German trauma centers have been able to save 25 percent of victims of would-be fatal auto accidents, which is close to the percentage of preventable deaths of American auto accident victims.

_____ **4.** If cigarettes burned more quickly, fewer fires would result from cigarettes being dropped by smokers who fall asleep with cigarettes in their hands.

_____ **5.** The use of motorcycle helmets and seat belts could save a significant number of lives each year.

_____ **6.** Stricter control of narcotic drug traffic would help to decrease drug-related crime.

_____ **7.** The United States needs to spend money and effort on studying ways to return trauma victims to being productive members of society.

_____ **8.** The United States has experimented with trauma centers in several of its major cities and has found them to be unsuccessful in terms of cost.

_____ **9.** Studies have been done which show that 30 percent to 40 percent of trauma-related deaths that occur in hospitals without trauma centers are preventable.

_____**10.** The United States should have learned from its own history in Korea and Vietnam the value of immediate professional medical care.

VOCABULARY FROM CONTEXT

Directions: *Using your own knowledge and information from the text, answer the following questions. Refer to the selection while you work. Don't be afraid to guess.*

1. intentional (paragraph 1)
   In this paragraph you see that injuries are "both accidental and intentional." *Both* lets you know that there are only two types of injuries being considered. If you are not hurt accidentally, then you are hurt intentionally.

   Intentional means _____.

2. respectively (paragraph 3)
   Read the sentence containing this word. By what percent has the

   death rate for heart disease fallen? _____ For stroke?

   _____

   Respectively means _____.

3. resuscitated (paragraph 7)

If a person considered "dead on arrival" when brought to the hospital later is well enough to go home, what happened when he or she was resuscitated?

Resuscitated means_____.

4. reversion (paragraph 9)

You know that words ending in *-ion* are nouns. What do you think

the verb of this word form is? _____

Reversion means _____.

5. advocates (paragraph 14)

If I am an advocate of handgun control, I will tell you that 11,000 of the 26,000 murders committed in 1982 involved handguns. If I am an opponent, I will give you the same statistic by saying that less than half of all murders in 1982 involved handguns.

Advocates means_____.

6. alleviated (paragraph 16)

Alleviated means _____.

What clues are there in the sentence itself and/or the paragraph?

_____

_____

SKILLS CHECKUP: CLASSIFICATION OF IDEAS

Directions: *Mark each sentence with one of the following letters to show how (or if) it supports the thesis statement: Major (M); Minor (m); Irrelevant (I).*

Thesis Statement: Although trauma clearly is a major medical and social problem in the United States, it is being neglected by physicians, hospital administrators, government officials, and the general public.

_____ **1.** Trauma is the leading cause of death among U.S. citizens under the age of 40.

_____ **2.** Auto accidents are responsible for 40 percent of the deaths among young whites.

_____ **3.** Most trauma-related deaths occur within a few hours of injury.

_____ **4.** Infection that sets in after an injury is responsible for a large percentage of late trauma-related deaths.

_____ **5.** West Germany has established an extensive network of trauma centers, which has greatly increased a trauma victim's chances for recovery.

_____ **6.** Because trauma primarily affects people at or near the beginning of their most productive work years, its cost measured in loss productivity is high.

_____ **7.** The total annual cost of accidental trauma, including lost wages, medical expenses, and indirect work losses, comes to about $50 billion.

_____ **8.** The only way to reduce the number of immediate deaths from accident or injury is through prevention.

_____ **9.** Increased urban violence has been a major contributor to the rise in homicide as a trauma factor.

_____**10.** Trauma patients currently take up a total of about 19 million hospital days per year in the United States.

_____**11.** Between 50 percent and 60 percent of the fatal motor-vehicle accidents in the United States are caused by drunk drivers.

_____**12.** Most hospital emergency rooms are not sufficiently prepared in terms of staffing and equipment to successfully meet the special needs of trauma victims.

_____**13.** Hospital administrators largely are unsupportive of high-cost programs, such as trauma centers.

_____**14.** There is a major shortfall in the delivery of trauma care in the United States.

_____**15.** A recent study of 71 motorcyclists injured while riding without helmets indicated that only 38 percent had medical insurance or workman's compensation; most of the unpaid bills were borne by the taxpayer.

SUMMARY

Directions: Fill in the blanks so that the following summary is logical, grammatically correct, and accurate according to the selection.

In his article entitled "_____," Donald Trunkey asserts that _____ trauma is a leading cause of injury and _____ in this country, it often is _____. Little attention has been given to _____ into its prevention. Trunkey, who _____ trauma as accidental or _____ personal injury, suggests five _____ aimed at the prevention of _____. First, _____ recommends the enactment of _____ intended to _____ the number of drunk _____ on the road, thereby _____ alcohol-related accidents. _____, Trunkey calls for laws _____ the use of auto safety _____ and motorcycle _____ in order to lessen the _____ and severity of injuries resulting from _____ accidents. Third, stricter _____ of the availability of handguns, he feels, would have a significant _____ on lowering the number of _____ resulting from _____ and intentional shootings. In addition, the author _____ that by making the _____ and possession of narcotic drugs _____, drug-related crimes would _____ and with them _____-related injury. Finally, he gives statistics to indicate that _____ injuries would be reduced if _____ makers would remove the incendiary _____ that cause cigarettes _____ less rapidly, thereby allowing them to burn themselves out before _____ a fire. With support of these proposed programs, Trunkey believes that a _____ percentage of personal injuries _____ be significantly reduced.

ESSAY QUESTIONS

Directions: *In one to three paragraphs, answer the following questions using information from the selection to support your ideas.*

1. The logic behind most of the trauma-prevention programs outlined by the author is clear. If we reduce the number of drunk drivers, we will reduce the number of injuries from alcohol-related traffic accidents. If people wear helmets and seat belts, the injuries from traffic accidents will be less severe, etc. But why does the author feel that the decriminalization of narcotics will aid in preventing trauma?

2. How does the author justify the cost of improving trauma care in the United States?

3. What kind of evidence (in terms of both money and lives lost) does Trunkey offer to demonstrate that trauma is a serious problem in the United States?

Theoretical Perspectives on Societies

5

Prereading

DISCUSSION

Directions: Read the following questions. Be prepared to discuss them.

1. This selection discusses two theories that describe the nature of societies: functionalism and conflict theory. Assuming that these are opposing theories, what do you think are the basic ideas behind each of them?

2. The selection describes an extended comparison, or metaphor, comparing society to a living organism. In what ways do you think a society is like a living thing?

3. What is the purpose of using citations, that is, giving authors' names and dates of their works, in a scholarly text?

4. Sociology is the study of society: its institutions, its groups, its relationships. What is the purpose of such study?

5. What are some things that hold a society together? What are some things that tear a society apart? Could issues that hold one society together tear another society apart? Give examples.

PREVIEW
PART 1: FUNCTIONALISM

Directions: Find the paragraph in which the following topics are discussed. Then write the number of the paragraph beside each topic.

_____ **a.** Functionalism has received some criticism.

_____ **b.** Functionalism is founded on biology.

_____ **c.** Examples of functional and dysfunctional societies are discussed.

_____ **d.** The definition of functionalism is given.

_____ **e.** A society must meet basic needs in order to be functional.

_____ **f.** A society has primary and secondary functions.

Now read the following phrases and sentences. Write the number of the paragraph in which you find each phrase or sentence.

_____ **a.** "Society is in many ways similar to a living organism."

_____ **b.** "Emile Durkheim is often thought of as the father of functionalism as we know it today."

_____ **c.** "The real functions of a unit of social structure may not be the same as its 'official,' or intended, functions."

_____ **d.** "The most forceful criticism . . . "

_____ **e.** "Charles Darwin . . . explain(ed) evolution in terms of natural selection."

PREVIEW
PART 2: CONFLICT THEORY

Directions: *Find the paragraph in which the following topics are discussed. Then write the number of the paragraph beside each topic.*

_____ **a.** Conflict theory may be explained in terms of Marxist sociology.

_____ **b.** A central part of conflict theory involves a power struggle between the strong and the weak.

_____ **c.** There are leaders within a society who dominate or rule that society.

_____ **d.** Many conflict theorists believe that societies are held together by force.

_____ **e.** There is a disagreement among conflict theorists.

_____ **f.** Even though there is much disagreement among sociologists, they agree that there is something important in each perspective of conflict theory as well as in functionalism.

Now read the following words, phrases, and sentences. Write the number of the paragraph in which you find each word, phrase, or sentence.

_____ **a.** "Conflict theory is not nearly so unified a viewpoint as functionalism."

_____ **b.** " . . . is that human beings are sociable but conflict-prone animals."

_____ **c.** "proletariat"

_____ **d.** "best-known book"

_____ **e.** "A major assumption"

_____ **f.** "Conflict theory, on the other hand, focuses on the strains and tensions in life."

READING

THEORETICAL PERSPECTIVES ON SOCIETIES

Now let us return to the two major theoretical perspectives on societies, functionalism **and** conflict theory. . . . *Here we shall explore these* perspectives in more detail and see how they are used to analyze the operation of societies.

Functionalism

1   Functionalism took on its basic form in the nineteenth century. In many ways, this was the century of biology. Knowledge of the human body, of microscopic forms of life, and of plants and animals around the world kept increasing. In one of the greatest achievements of the century, Charles Darwin drew on this vast body of new knowledge to explain evolution in terms of natural selection. Biology had never before enjoyed such high prestige. Excited by these steps forward, social thinkers naturally began to apply some of the concepts of biology to society.

2   Auguste Comte and Herbert Spencer proposed the most basic idea of functionalism: *Society is in many ways similar to a living organism.* There are three aspects of this idea: First, society, like a living thing, has structure. An animal is made up of cells, tissues, and organs; society is likewise made up of structures such as groups, classes, and institutions. Second, like an organism, society is a system that has certain needs to be satisfied if the system is to survive. Societies must, for example, be able to get food and resources from the surroundings and distribute them to their members. Third, like the parts of a biological organism, the parts of a social system seem to work together in an orderly way to maintain the well-being of the whole. Spencer and his followers said that the natural tendency of systems is toward equilibrium or stability, and that each part of society has a function that adds to this stability. Thus, in formal terms functionalism views society as a complex system made up of parts that function to fulfill the needs of the whole so as to maintain stability.

3   Later, scholars took the basic idea of functionalism—that society is similar to a living organism—and refined and added to it. Émile Durkheim is often thought of as the father of functionalism as we know it today.

Source: David Popenoe, *Sociology,* © 1983, pp. 93–96. Reprinted by permission of Prentice-Hall, Englewood Cliffs, New Jersey.

In his work he made heavy use of functionalist terms drawn from biology. He saw society as a special kind of organism, one ruled by a consensus of moral values. Functionalism was also the major perspective of the British founders of the branch of anthropology called "cultural anthropology."

4   In the United States, the sociologist Talcott Parsons was the leading figure in making functionalism into a general yet systematic theory for sociological analysis. A society, he said, will remain functional—that is, maintain its order and stability—if it can meet four basic needs (Parsons, 1951; Parsons & Smelser, 1956). These four needs, sometimes called *functional requisites*, are the achievement of goals, adjustment to the environment, the integration of the various parts of society into a whole, and control of deviance from accepted norms. Parsons (1951) placed special emphasis on the need to integrate the parts of a society, which he felt required that people believe in and follow their society's *shared values*. These shared values, he said, serve as a kind of "glue" holding society together. If too many people reject these values, social stability will break down.

5   Robert Merton (1968) refined Parsons' functionalism and made it more useful for guiding empirical research. He began by focusing on the function of a given unit of social structure. Earlier theorists often explained the presence of a part by saying that it adds to the maintenance of the whole. It was difficult, however, for them to see any social unit as harmful to the whole. If a unit of social structure existed, they thought, it must be functional. But Merton pointed out that not all parts of a social system need be functional. A unit of structure is *dysfunctional* when it prevents society, or one of its parts, from meeting its needs.

6   Religion is functional when it binds together the members of a society; an army is functional when it protects a society from harm; a political machine is functional when it helps to integrate immigrant groups into a society by providing them with needed information about government and social services. But religion that promotes political strife, as in Northern Ireland, is dysfunctional. So are an army that drains resources from other pressing social needs, such as health or education, and a political machine that relies on graft and creates corruption in public life.

7   It is also important to point out that the "real" functions of a unit of social structure may not be the same as its "official," or intended, functions. Besides its intended or **manifest functions**, a unit of social structure also has unrecognized, unintended **latent functions**.

8   One manifest function (intended purpose) of colleges and universities, for instance, is to educate young people and prepare them for specialized roles in society. A latent function (unintended purpose) may be to keep a large part of the population (students) out of the job market and so prevent strains on the economy.

9   Functionalism has been criticized on many grounds, but mainly that its view of society is inherently conservative. Because it stresses shared values and views society as composed of parts that function together for the benefit of the whole, functionalism seems to leave little room for people who do not share society's values or who try to change them. Critics charge that it gives little attention to dissent and social conflict. By focusing so heavily on order, stability, and consensus, functionalism may even distort the true nature of societies.

Unlike the parts of an organism, argue the critics, the parts of society do not always function together for the benefit of the whole. Some societal parts are in conflict; some parts benefit at the expense of others.

10   The most forceful criticism of functional theory has come from a group called conflict theorists. They agree that the functional perspective may be valuable in studying stable societies. But a look around the world today suggests that societies are rising and falling at a rapid rate, and conflict is not the exception but the rule.

Conflict Theory

11   *Conflict theory* is not nearly so unified a viewpoint as functionalism. It is, instead, a varied body of theories that has been given the conflict label only in recent years. Perhaps the one common belief of all conflict theorists is that societies are always in a state of conflict over scarce resources. One of the most important scarce resources is power. Therefore, conflict theorists argue, society is best viewed as an arena in which there is a constant struggle for power.

12   A major assumption of many conflict theorists is that, rather than being held together by the "glue" of shared values, societies and social order are maintained by force. The more powerful members of society are able, partly through the use of force, to get the less powerful members of the society to conform to their values. One of the main concerns of conflict theorists, therefore, has been to pick out the dominant groups in society and to discover how they maintain their dominance—and, in fact, how they achieved their power in the first place.

13   Sometimes "conflict theory" means simply Marxist sociology. Marxist sociologists emphasize economic forces in societies, in contrast to functionalism's emphasis on shared cultural values. And they stress the constant struggle between economic classes of people. Marx identified two classes: the working class, or *proletariat*, and the owners of the means of production, or *bourgeoisie*. He predicted that the conflict between these two classes would lead to the revolutionary overthrow of capitalist societies, with classless society as the final outcome (Marx, 1848). That this prediction has not yet come to pass, however, does not mean that the basic class struggle has ended in most capitalist societies. Neo-Marxist conflict theorists continue to follow Marx in emphasizing that most societies are torn by conflict and struggle between economic classes. They say that social progress will occur only when the power of the capitalists—the dominant class—is diminished (Braverman, 1974).

14   But the term "conflict theory" typically includes many non-Marxist sociologists as well. Perhaps the best known of living conflict theorists is the German sociologist Ralf Dahrendorf (1958, 1959), who is now head of the London School of Economics. Dahrendorf attacks the basic premise of functionalism, that society is orderly. He regards that premise as almost utopian (1958) and directs attention to society's "ugly face"—that of conflict. In contrast to Marx, he sees conflict as more a struggle for power than a class conflict over

economic resources. But like Marx, he views society as always verging on instability and change. Indeed, he maintains that the study of social change, not social order, should be the main focus in the analysis of society (1959).

15   The founding father of conflict theory in the United States was C. Wright Mills. Mills felt that he was working in a Marxist tradition, but there is also much in his thought that comes from the work of Max Weber. In addition, Mills's work comes out of midwestern populism and its battle against the "big interests" in American life. In his best-known book, *The Power Elite* (1956), Mills tried to discover who really rules in America. He concluded that America is dominated by leaders from three spheres that are more and more related: top management of the big corporations, key officials in government, and the top ranks of the military. Moreover, these leaders are easily interchanged. Corporate executives often join the government, and retired generals are elected to the boards of large corporations. Thus, Mills felt, a small and very centralized group makes most of the major decisions in our society about war and peace, money and taxes, civil rights and responsibilities.

16   The ideas developed by Mills are central to much of conflict theory today (e.g., Domhoff, 1967, 1978, 1980). Despite their visible signs of success, conflict theorists note, the people who make up the "power elite" are often less aware of their power than they are of other people's resistance to it. To deal with this resistance and to keep public resentment within bounds, those in power try to blur the line between themselves and the masses. Nonetheless, the masses are aware of their powerlessness, and they resent it. The ten-

sion between the strong and the weak becomes the breeding ground for social conflict. The people who benefit most from the social order as it is will seek to preserve it. Those who are deprived will work to change it. And the conflict resulting from the opposition of these groups can lead to radical social change.

17   An important younger theorist closely connected with the conflict perspective is Randall Collins. Collins clearly sees himself following in the footsteps of Max Weber, who strongly opposed Karl Marx on many issues. The basic insight of conflict theory, Collins says, "is that human beings are sociable but conflict-prone animals" (1975, p. 59). The term "conflict theory" also has been used to refer to the work of scholars such as Lewis Coser (1956, 1967). (Coser, however, rejects the label.) Building on the work of Georg Simmel, Coser has studied the process of social conflict in all its forms. He has not tried to develop a "theory of society."

18   Conflict theories differ among themselves not only in what areas of social conflict they choose to emphasize but also in their views on the role of social science in society (Wallace & Wolf, 1980). Some conflict theorists, especially those working in the Marxist tradition, feel a moral obligation not only to criticize society but also actively to promote social change. These sociologists reject the principle of ethical neutrality, ... the principle that social scientists should do only scientific work and not fight political and moral battles. Other conflict theorists—such as Ralf Dahrendorf, Randall Collins, and Lewis Coser—hold a more traditional view. They feel that the main aim of the social services is explanation rather than social activism and that social scientists must strive to be

objective about political events.

19   The issue of the role of the social sciences in society provokes some of the most bitter debate between conflict theorists (at least those who reject the principle of ethical neutrality) and functionalists. Otherwise, most sociologists today, no matter what their own views, accept that each perspective has something important to offer—that each is looking at a different aspect of society. Functionalism looks at the way people work together in everyday life. It gives some important answers to the question: Why are people who have their own special needs and interests often so cooperative with one another? Conflict theory, on the other hand, focuses on the strains and tensions in life, on the lack of equality in societies, and on breakdowns in social order. Just as functionalism may sometimes err in seeing more cooperation and order than actually exists, conflict theories may err in seeing social conflict as *the* major form of social interaction. But both perspectives point up aspects of our social existence that are basic and universal, as we will explore further in many of the chapters to follow.

References

Braverman, H. 1975. *Labor and Monopoly Capital.* New York: Monthly Review Press

Collins, Randall. 1975. *Conflict Sociology.* Orlando, FL: Academic Press

Coser, Lewis. 1956. *The Functions of Social Conflict.* New York: Free Press

Coser, Lewis. 1967. *Continuities in the Study of Social Conflict.* New York: Free Press

Dahrendorf, Ralf. 1958. "Out of utopia: Toward a reorganization of sociological analysis." *American Journal of Sociology* 64:115–127

Dahrendorf, Ralf. 1959. *Class and Class Conflict in Industrial Society.* Palo Alto, CA: Stanford University Press

Domhoff, G. William, 1967. *Who Rules America?* Englewood Cliffs, NJ: Prentice-Hall

Domhoff, G. William. 1978. *Who Really Rules?* New Brunswick, NJ: Transaction Books

Domhoff, G. William (ed.). 1980. *Power Structure Research.* Beverly Hills: Sage

Marx, Karl, and Friedrich Engels. 1969. *The Communist Manifesto.* Baltimore: Penguin Books. (Originally published in 1848.)

Merton, Robert K. 1968. *Social Theory and Social Structure* (enl. ed.). New York: Free Press

Mills, C. Wright. 1956. *The Power Elite.* New York: Oxford University Press

Parsons, Talcott. 1951. *The Social System.* Glencoe, IL: Free Press

Parsons, Talcott, and Neil J. Smelser. 1956. *Economy and Society.* New York: Free Press

Wallace, R., and A. Wolf. 1980. *Contemporary Sociological Theory.* Englewood Cliffs, NJ: Prentice-Hall

—From David Popenoe, *Sociology.* Prentice-Hall, 1983.

Postreading

TRUE OR FALSE

Directions: Decide if each of the following statements is true (T) or false (F) based on the selection.

_____ **1.** Sociologists have been influenced by theories in biology.

_____ **2.** Karl Marx believed that society is similar to a living organism.

_____ **3.** "Stability" is the foundation of conflict theory as we know it today.

_____ **4.** While many sociologists in the United States explained societies in terms of functionalism, cultural anthropologists in England attempted to explain societies in terms of conflict theory.

_____ **5.** The four functional requisites are obtaining goals, adjusting to the environment, integrating the various parts of society into a whole, and controlling the less powerful members of a society.

_____ **6.** An example of a dysfunctional structure in society is a military which uses up the money necessary for social welfare programs.

_____ **7.** A latent function is one that is unknown to the members of society.

_____ **8.** Most conflict theorists believe that societies are always struggling over scarce resources.

_____ **9.** *Bourgeoisie* refers to the working class of people and *proletariat* refers to the owners of production.

_____ **10.** As Marx predicted, the conflict between the workers and owners of production resulted in an overthrow of the capitalist society in England, leaving a classless society.

_____ **11.** Social change, according to conflict theorists, is due to instability caused by conflict.

_____ **12.** Conflict theorists view members of societies as independent whereas functionalists view them as being dependent on one another.

READING WORKSHEET

Directions: After you have completed the true-or-false exercise, answer the following questions. You may refer to the selection if necessary.

1. What is the purpose of paragraph 1? _____

    _____

2. In the last sentence of paragraph 1, what does *these steps forward*

    refer to? _____

    _____

3. Why is functionalism described in terms of biology? _____

    _____

4. In the definition of functionalism given in the text, what are the

    "parts" that make up a society? _____

    _____

5. How did Émile Durkheim's idea of functionalism differ from those

    of Auguste Compte and Herbert Spencer? _____

    _____

6. Paragraphs 2 through 5 are related to a particular sentence in

    paragraph 1. Which sentence is it and what is its function? _____

    _____

7. Who was Talcott Parsons? _____

    _____

8. According to Parsons, what needs must be met in order to maintain

    a functional society? _____

    _____

9. How did Robert Merton's theory of functionalism differ from that of Parsons'? _____

_____

10. What is the purpose of paragraph 6? _____

_____

11. What is the major topic discussed in paragraph 6? _____

_____

12. What is the meaning of the prefix *dys-*? _____

13. In your own words, define *latent function* and *manifest function*. Give an example of each. _____

_____

14. According to functionalist theory, what is the major purpose of a society? _____

_____

15. What relationship do paragraphs 9 and 10 have to the next section of the reading, "Conflict Theory"? _____

_____

16. Whereas functional theorists believe society is held together by "glue," conflict theorists believe society is held together by _____

_____

17. According to conflict theorists, what causes conflict within a society?

_____

_____

18. In the phrase *to get the less powerful members of the societies to conform to their values* (paragraph 12), what does *their* refer to? _____

_____

19. According to Karl Marx, where does the main conflict in society lie?

_____

_____

_____

20. In your own words, what does Marx think will happen to capitalist societies? _____

21. In paragraph 13, why are the terms *proletariat* and *bourgeoisie* in italics? _____

_____

22. What type of organization is used in the discussion of Mills's conflict theory?
   a. comparison/contrast
   b. cause and effect
   c. chronological order
   d. all of the above
   e. both b and c

23. In *The people who benefit most from the social order as it is will seek to preserve it* (paragraph 16), what does *it* refer to? _____

_____

24. What "positive" feature of society has Randall Collins attributed to conflict theory? _____

_____

25. In what ways do conflict theories differ among themselves? _____

_____

INFERENCE AND RESTATEMENT

Directions: *Decide whether each of the following is a restatement (R), an inference (I), or false statement (F) according to the selection. If the sentence is a restatement, locate the original in the selection and give the paragraph number where it is found.*

_____ **1.** Sociologists have developed two major theories concerning the relationship among groups within a society.

_____ **2.** Functionalism takes a kinder view of human societies than does conflict theory.

_____ **3.** Dissent is an important element of all societies that all sociological theories consider.

_____ **4.** Marxist sociologists do not believe that capitalism is a workable system because it forces individuals or groups to compete for resources needed by all the members of a society.

_____ **5.** It is the understood primary objective of a university to provide the opportunity for higher education to the population.

_____ **6.** According to conflict theory, powerful people who desire to keep their power want less powerful people to be aware of it and to respect it.

_____ **7.** According to conflict theory, the people who have the most power are those who have the support of groups that control the resources of the society.

_____ **8.** According to C. Wright Mills, decisions about important matters that affect the society as a whole often are made by the most powerful group.

_____ **9.** According to conflict theory, the natural tendency of society is toward stability.

_____**10.** The focus of conflict theory is the struggle between those who have power and those who do not.

OUTLINING

Directions: *Below is a partial outline of the "Functionalism" section from the selection. Reread that section and complete the outline.*

I. Functionalism

    **Defines society as _____

    _____.

    A. _____

        _____

        _____

        1. _____

        2. Both have certain needs that must be fulfilled.

        3. _____

    B. Émile Durkheim, the father of functionalism, says society is ruled by a consensus of moral values.

    C. Talcott Parsons _____

        _____.

        1. _____

        2. _____

        3. _____

        4. Control of deviance

    D. _____

        _____ dysfunctional parts of society.

        1. _____ aspects of society

          a. Religion: _____

          b. Military: protecting society

          c. _____

        2. Dysfunctional _____

          a. _____

          b. _____

          c. _____: creating corruption

VOCABULARY FROM CONTEXT

Directions: *Using your own knowledge and information from the text, answer the following questions. Refer to the selection while you work. Don't be afraid to guess.*

1. prestige (paragraph 1)
   Notice the tone of this sentence (*enjoyed, high*).

   Prestige means _____.

2. dissent (paragraph 9)
   In this line, the word is linked to social conflict.

   Dissent means _____.

3. verging (paragraph 14)
   Like Karl Marx, Ralf Dahrendorf sees society as constantly "verging on instability and change." Look at Marx's theory in paragraph 13. Notice the words *predicted* and *lead*.

   Verging means _____.

4. to blur the line (paragraph 16)
   If an important powerful person wants to win the sympathy and support of the powerless people, will he make a sharp distinction between himself and potential supporters?

   To blur the line means _____.

5. provokes (paragraph 19)
   What in the organization of the sentence gives you a clue to the meaning of this word?

   Provokes means _____

   _____.

6. strains (paragraph 19)

   Strains means _____.
   How do you know? What clues are there in the sentence itself

   and/or the paragraph? _____

   _____

SUMMARY

Directions: Fill in the blanks so that the following summary is logical, grammatically correct, and accurate according to the selection.

Two major theoretical _____ on societies are _____ and conflict _____. Functionalism is based on the _____ of society to a living _____. The complex parts of a _____ function to maintain its order and stability through the fulfillment of four basic _____ called functional _____. Sometimes, a part of the _____ structure may become _____—that is, it upsets rather than _____ order. Some sociologists feel that _____ is unrealistic because it does not deal with those who do not agree with society's _____. Conflict theory holds the view that _____ are in a state of constant _____ over scarce _____. According to many _____, the dominant groups in a society maintain control and get _____ powerful groups to conform to their norms by _____. One major focus of conflict theory is to identify these _____ groups and to find out what causes this imbalance of _____. Most conflict theorists believe that society is always on the edge of _____, perhaps even revolution because of this imbalance.

ESSAY QUESTIONS

Directions: In one to three paragraphs, answer the following questions using information from the selection to support your ideas.

1. Compare and contrast the basic ideas of Dahrendorf's conflict theory with those of Marx.

2. What are the three dominating groups discussed in Mills's *The Power Elite*? How are these three groups related?

3. How can functionalism and conflict theory interact to explain the structure of a society?

RELATED READING

Aging and the Social Structure: The Functionalist Perspective

From a functionalist perspective the kind of socialization that the older person experiences depends a great deal on the way a society is structured and how it values the qualities and attributes of an older person. The biological changes that go with aging—such as weakened muscles, diminished use of senses, sometimes senility—do not differ from society to society. Societies do differ, however, in how they regard these natural changes. Nomadic peoples, constantly on the move and dependent on scarce resources, consider old people a burden (Sheehan, 1976). In agricultural societies, on the other hand, the aged enjoy great prestige, derived from their years of experience and wisdom in the ways of planting and harvesting and their accumulation of property over their lifetime. In such a society, it quite literally pays to give deference to the aged.

Modern industrial society grants little status to old people. In fact, such a society has a system of built-in obsolescence. We get educated in our youth, but no formal system exists for continuing our education throughout our life in order to keep up with rapidly changing knowledge. "People whose education and job skills have grown obsolete are treated exactly like those who have never gained an education or job skills and are not encouraged or given the opportunity to begin anew" (Atchley, 1980, p. 16).

As a society becomes more highly developed the overall status of older people diminishes (Atchley, 1980; see Table 5–1). Improved health technology creates a large pool of old people, who compete for jobs with younger people. However, economic technology lowers the demand for workers and creates new jobs for which the skills of the aged are obsolete, forcing old people into retirement. At the same time, young people are being educated in the new technology and are keeping pace with rapid changes in knowledge. Finally, urbanization creates age-segregated neighborhoods. Because the old live on fixed incomes, they must often live in inferior housing. All these factors—retirement, obsolete knowledge and skills, inferior standards of living—lower the status of the aged in our society.

It appears that our life span outpaces our usefulness in society today. A century ago, when one could expect to live only to age 50 or so, the life span more or less coincided with the occupation and family cycle. But today the average life span allows for fifteen to twenty years of life *after* these cycles.

TABLE 5–1   Personal Qualities of Older People

Personal Quality	"Most People Over 65" as Seen by Public 18 to 64 (Percent)	"Most People Over 65" as Seen by Public 65 and Over (Percent)	Self-Image of Public 18 to 64 (Percent)	Self-Image of Public 65 and Over (Percent)
Very friendly and warm	82	25	63	72
Very wise from experience	66	56	54	69
Very bright and alert	29	33	73	68
Very open-minded and adaptable	19	34	67	63
Very good at getting things done	35	38	60	55
Very physically active	41	43	65	48
Very sexually active	5	6	47	11

Source: From *The Social Forces in Later Life: An Introduction to Social Gerontology*, Third Edition, by Robert C. Atchley; © 1980 by Wadsworth, Inc. Reprinted by permission of the publisher.

* * *

The stereotype the general public holds of old people often does not accord with old people's images of themselves. For example, while only 19 percent of people under sixty-five see old people as very open-minded and adaptable, a much larger proportion—34 percent—of old people hold that others in their age group are. And when old people rate themselves as individuals, an even greater proportion (63 percent) considers themselves open-minded and adaptable.

* * *

Following the functionalist perspective to its conclusion can result in a very pessimistic view of the position of the aged in modern American society. Sociologist Irving Rosow (1974) sees social changes as undermining all the major determinants of older people's status—property ownership, strategic knowledge, productivity, mutual dependence, tradition and religion, kinship and family, and community life.

However, the degree to which an old person loses status depends on his or her individual circumstances. Old people with a good retirement pension will obviously adjust more easily than those with an inadequate pension. A widow or widower is more likely to say that old age is lonely than an intact couple. It is important, then, to look at the resources and the roles that belong to a particular person.

—From Donald Light, Jr., and Suzanne Keller, *Sociology*, Third Edition, © 1982, Alfred A. Knopf, Inc.

DISCUSSION

Directions: *Read the following questions. Be prepared to discuss them.*

1. Give examples of how attitudes toward aging differ from society to society.

2. Why are older people considered "dysfunctional" in modern societies?

3. How do many societies make it difficult for older people to be functional?

4. What problems do older people face in your native country? Analyze these problems from a functionalist standpoint.

5. Look at Table 5–1 and answer the following questions.
   What personal qualities are being analyzed?
   Who was involved in this study?
   What kind of stereotypes does the public, age 18 to 64, have about the aged?
   How does the public, age 64 and over, feel about themselves?
   We can see a gap in the views between the age groups. What do you think this gap means in a society?

6. What are some things that could be done to improve the position of older people in society?

6 The Cigarette Century

Prereading

DISCUSSION

Directions: Read the following questions. Be prepared to discuss them.

1. Have you ever smoked? When did you start smoking? Why did you start? If you have never smoked, what stopped you from starting?

2. If you smoke, have you ever tried to stop smoking and failed? What did you do? What was the experience like?

3. Why do you think that some people can stop smoking easily while others can't?

4. Are people's smoking habits changing in your country? Are more or fewer people smoking? Are more or fewer women smoking?

5. Is smoking considered a "normal" activity in your country or is it "unusual"?

PREVIEW

Directions: Read the title and any subheadings of the selection. Also look at the illustrations and read any captions. Then, without reading the selection, answer the following questions.

1. Who is the author of the selection and what are his credentials?

2. What do you think is the author's purpose in writing this selection?

3. Who is the intended audience?

4. Mark the following statements as true or false based on your inferences about the content of the selection.

   _____ **a.** As soon as cigarettes began to be produced by a machine, more people began to smoke.

_____ **b.** Cigarette smoking is a completely physiological addiction.

_____ **c.** Cigarettes are big business in the United States.

_____ **d.** Cigars are more addictive than cigarettes.

5. Underline the first sentence of each paragraph. Then read only those sentences. Next decide where the topics change throughout the reading. Complete the chart below.

Paragraph	Topic
4	an inventor and his invention
_____	historical perspective
_____	nicotine and addiction
_____	cigarettes as big business
_____	conclusion

READING

THE CIGARETTE CENTURY

How a clever invention kicked off an epidemic of addiction.

by WILLIAM BENNETT, M.D.

1   Eli Whitney, Thomas Alva Edison, Henry Ford, Alexander Graham Bell, James Bonsack, Wilbur and . . .

2   Wait a minute. *James Bonsack?*

3   Yes, James Albert Bonsack of Roanoke County, Virginia.

4   Although he has left but a faint trace in the history books, Bonsack belongs to the list of American tinkers and inventors who made an indelible mark on modern civilization. Just a hundred years ago—on September 4, 1880, to be precise—Bonsack filed for a patent on his design of a cigarette-rolling machine. Bonsack's complicated but clever invention made cheap cigarettes a possibility; and before long a new type of tobacco made them a necessity for millions of people.

5   Until the 1870s, manufactured cigarettes were a minor item—a kind of dandified luxury—in the American tobacco trade. In 1869, fewer than two million were produced, all of them hand-rolled. But demand soon began to increase, and in 1875 the firm of Allen & Ginter offered a prize of $75,000 for a machine to do the job.

6   James Bonsack, a gifted teenager well acquainted with the machinery in his family's woolen mill, set out to win the award. He interrupted his efforts only briefly to attend Roanoke College, then dropped out, over his father's protests, to keep working on the invention. A month before his twenty-first birthday, James filed for his first patent. The "Bonsack," as his machine came to be known, poured a uniform

Until the 1880s, experts rolled cigarettes by hand at the rate of 40 a minute. (Culver Pictures, Inc.)

flow of tobacco through a device resembling the wool feeder of a carding machine onto a thin strip of paper. The paper was rolled into a single, continuous tube. As it emerged from the machine, the tobacco-filled tube was cut into equal lengths.

7   The machine worked. It was improved. Father and son reconciled and set up a joint stock company to produce more machines and lease them to tobacco firms.

8   In retrospect, it seems surprising that there was a market for cigarettes. In the United States, per capita consumption of tobacco products had fallen for nearly a century, and it appears to have reached an all-time low of 1.8 pounds in the early 1870s. And yet, even in the decade before Bonsack filed for his patent, demand for cigarettes grew some thirtyfold. Why did a waning vice, subject to a good deal of mid-Victorian opprobrium, suddenly reestablish itself? And why did the impoverished tobacco country of Piedmont Virginia and North Carolina—now known as the "Old Bright Belt," where most cigarette tobacco is grown—rapidly become one of the most prosperous agricultural regions of the world?

9   Fairly abruptly, after the Civil War, methods of tobacco processing changed in the Old Bright Belt. As a result, smoke from the tobacco grown there became relatively easy to inhale, and nicotine, when delivered by inhalation, is a highly addicting substance. The cigarette happens to be the ideal means for obtaining manageable doses of inhaled nicotine. Mechanization, clever advertising and marketing techniques made their contribution, but they never would have sold much dried cabbage.

10   *Nicotiana* is an American plant that was transported around the world by the European explorers. When the Jamestown colonists arrived in the New World a century after Columbus, they brought the tobacco habit back with them. But where they settled they found an altogether harsh-tasting species of tobacco—just one more hardship in a generally tough existence. Then, about 1612, John Rolfe imported seed of a milder variety from one of Spain's Caribbean colonies. This tobacco did well in the sandy Virginia soil, and within a few years its smoking qualities were improved when a neighbor of Rolfe's began to cure his leaves by hanging them instead of stacking them on the ground. Curing

is a process in which harvested tobacco is slowly dried; it removes excess starch and permits other chemical reactions, which lead to a milder smoke. The quality of the smoke is very sensitive to the rate and temperature of curing.

11   Tobacco grown in the Old Bright Belt became known for its mildness—mainly a result of the nitrogen-poor soil—but not until the 19th century did improvements in curing methods yield a leaf with smoke mild enough to be routinely inhaled. The first steps were made when it was discovered that heating tobacco at just the right time turns the leaf a bright yellow (hence the name "bright" tobacco), a color associated with a mild and pleasant smoke. Open flames of wood or charcoal were used for the purpose at first, but they imparted their own flavor to the curing leaves.

12   In the early 1800s, a few attempts were made to isolate wood smoke from the tobacco by building fires in furnaces outside the curing barns and leading the heat in through flues. That method was unsuccessful mainly because construction of the ducts was clumsy, and disastrous fires often destroyed barn and crop.

13   Safely designed flues, developed immediately after the Civil War, made all the difference. With flue curing, mild bright tobacco could be reliably turned out, and by 1880, as demand continually grew for the resulting product, this method became standard in the Old Bright Belt. What the tobacco growers and manufacturers could not have known was that the change in curing method

Kentucky burley tobacco—one of Kentucky's largest industries. (Courtesy of Kentucky Department of Travel Development)

had significantly altered the chemistry of their product. The smoke was not only mild it was slightly acid instead of alkaline. Thus, the tobacco that was poured into Bonsack's new machines, and has been the chief component of cigarettes ever since, was unlike virtually any that had been available earlier, and the slight shift from alkaline to acid smoke

for absorption to occur. On the lungs' vast surface the acidity is neutralized; the nicotine loses its electric charge and passes rapidly into the bloodstream.

16 From the lungs, nicotine-loaded blood is carried back to the heart, which gives a squeeze and sends about 15 percent of the inhaled dose directly, and undiluted, to the brain. The brain, in

government study, have only a 15 percent chance of remaining nonsmokers. And when, after years of smoking people try to kick the habit, they suffer from physical and psychological symptoms that persist for at least a couple of weeks, and some of their afflictions, including drowsiness and craving, usually get worse after ten days or so. For most, craving

Smoking a cigarette will never again be regarded as normal behavior.

radically changed the nature of the smoking habit.

14 Nicotine passes easily through living tissue only when it is in an alkaline medium. Under even slightly acid conditions, virtually every molecule of nicotine carries an electric charge that prevents it from crossing membranes. Pipe and cigar tobaccos, cured by age-old methods, yield an alkaline smoke, from which nicotine can be gradually absorbed in modest quanitities through the mucous membranes of the mouth. The alkalinity itself makes the smoke irritating and deters inhalation.

15 By contrast, the slight acidity of cigarette smoke is not readily neutralized by saliva, so relatively little nicotine can be absorbed if the smoke is just held in the mouth. But because cigarette smoke is not highly irritating it can be drawn into the lungs—indeed, it must be

turn, takes up on the first pass virtually all of the nicotine carried to it. The whole journey takes seven seconds. In comparison, heroin injected into the forearm takes about 14 seconds to reach the brain, and on its way, the dose becomes diluted by blood from other parts of the body.

17 Conventional explanations of cigarette smoking have called it a form of psychological dependence, in which the child's pacifier and security blanket are rolled into one little white tube for grown-up use. There is some reason to believe that pipe and cigar smoking reflect more a psychological need than a physiological one. But the cigarette habit is extremely potent and often very difficult either to give up or substitute with other crutches. Adolescents who smoke more than one cigarette, according to a British

persists at least a month, and for about a fifth it continues five to nine *years* after they quit.

18 Only recently, with the work of British psychiatrist Michael A. H. Russell of the Maudsley Hospital in London, American psychologist Stanley Schachter of Columbia University, and other investigators, has the addictive nature of nicotine been clarified. By now there is little doubt that the drug, absorbed in the right way, creates a state of drug dependency. Confusion on the point arose and has persisted because nicotine is not like many other addicting substances: It does not interfere with "normal" behavior and thinking. Quite the contrary, cigarette smokers report that they need to smoke in order to focus their attention, to avoid drowsiness and a sense of blurred consciousness. The objective

changes associated with smoking are also those of increased arousal, even though most smokers report the subjective effect as relaxation. In general, nicotine resembles stimulants, such as caffeine and amphetamine, more than the narcotics.

19   Russell hypothesizes that nicotine becomes highly addictive only when it is inhaled. What an inhaling cigarette smoker receives from his or her habit is a series of nicotine jolts, and the smoker seeks the jolts for two reasons. First, they give an ill-defined, but generally pleasurable sensation, and the average cigarette smoker can easily obtain 70,000 to 100,000 fixes a year—two to three hundred each day. Such frequent rewards serve as powerful reinforcers of cigarette-smoking behavior. Second, administering nicotine in brief, concentrated jolts is the best way to keep high levels in the brain—more so even than intravenous injection, which inevitably results in dilution of the dose.

20   Nicotine addiction requires the smoker to accept a certain compromise, however. At the same time that the addict wants to raise brain levels of nicotine, he or she must guard against elevated levels elsewhere in the body, lest nausea and wooziness result from peripheral effects of the drug. Even though smokers become metabolically accustomed to nicotine, they have their limits. Indeed, most seem to be more careful to keep themselves below a maximum level of blood nicotine than above a minimum.

21   But as blood levels fall, so do brain levels; and withdrawal sets in. Beginning as craving and irritability, nicotine withdrawal proceeds to a panoply of physiological as well as psychological symptoms. Brain wave patterns change, levels of certain hormones diminish, heart rate and blood pressure fall. Abstinent smokers often complain of nausea, headache, constipation or diarrhea. They gain weight. Inability to concentrate is perhaps the most common and persistent subjective complaint, and it is accompanied by objective deficits in performance of tasks that require vigilance or tracking.

22   Once the smoking habit is well established, preventing withdrawal becomes the major motivation for continuing it, as Schachter showed in a series of studies conducted at Columbia during the 1970s. He found that chronic smokers are not made less irritable than other people by their habit; rather, they are protected from becoming more irritable. In one of his more naturalistic experiments conducted by Deborah Perlick, subjects sat in a laboratory decorated to look like a living room in Queens and listened to recordings of airplanes passing overhead. Allowed to smoke at will, they responded just like nonsmokers to the roaring and screeching. But kept from smoking or allowed to smoke only low-nicotine cigarettes, they became much more annoyed than before, and more so than nonsmokers. Schachter concluded from this experiment, and others using such irritants as electric shocks, that chronic cigarette smokers maintain their habit not for any pleasure it adds to their lives, though they may rationalize that they do, but rather to avoid the unpleasantness that comes from not smoking.

23   The rate at which a person smokes seems to be largely determined by the rate at which nicotine levels fall, and a major variable affecting the rate of nicotine removal from the body is the acidity of the urine. At any given moment, about a third of the nicotine molecules in the blood do not carry an electric charge; they pass freely through membranes, and that is how they travel into the urine. If the urine is even slightly acid, the nicotine is immediately charged and thus trapped; it cannot freely return to the bloodstream as it would if the urine were alkaline.

24   The times when smokers are most likely to light up are quite predictably those times when urine is acid. Psychological stress, for example, acidifies the urine. So do cocktail parties. So does eating; urine is distinctly acid for half an hour or so after a meal. The one major exception to the rule appears to be morning. Al-

The Dukes of Durham were among the first manufacturers of cigarettes in America, and in 1890, they became the only ones when they founded the American Tobacco Co. (Division of Archives and History, State of North Carolina)

though urine is acid in the morning smokers often do not smoke until later in the day. There probably are two reasons for this paradox: Most smokers are more sensitive to side-effects of nicotine in the morning, and those who want to cut down do so by postponing the first cigarette of the day.

25   As many as 90 percent of cigarette smokers, by some estimates, would like to cut down, or quit, and many have. The reason for quitting is also the reason why it is so difficult to quit. Cigarette smoke is inhaled, and inhaled tobacco smoke can be lethal.

26   But nobody knew that a hundred years ago, least of all James Buchanan Duke, the real father of the American cigarette industry. Duke began his career in the tobacco trade in 1865, at the age of nine. That year, his father, Washington Duke, a reluctant Confederate soldier who had been opposed to slavery, returned from the war to find his farm despoiled of everything except —miraculously—a barn full of bright yellow tobacco laid down before he left for duty. With his family's help, the elder Duke pulverized the tobacco, packed it in large muslin bags stenciled with his new brand name "Pro Bono Publico" and loaded the bags on a wagon. Then he harnessed two blind mules that he bought on leaving the army and set out with his son to sell the tobacco. It was good stuff, and they came home with enough money to stay in business.

27   The Duke concern grew, and at the age of 18, Buck, as the boy was known, became a partner. After ten years of selling its smoking tobacco, the Duke firm was substantial but hardly in a league with its chief competitor, Bull Durham, so Duke began manufacturing cigarettes. He leased several Bonsacks, installed the machines, improved them, and began to undersell other manufacturers. In 1889, W.

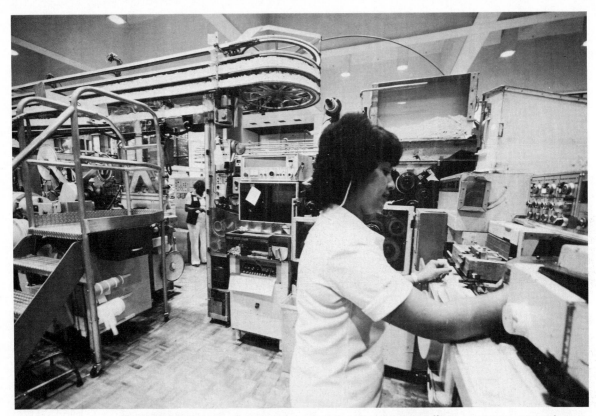

At a Philip Morris plant, an operator monitors the quality assurance computer as the cigarette making machine turns out more than 4,200 cigarettes a minute. (John Marmaras/Woodfin Camp)

Duke & Sons sold a billion cigarettes, 40 percent of the country's output. And one year later, Duke, who never smoked his product, took over the United States' entire cigarette industry. His monopoly, The American Tobacco Company, survived until 1911, when the Supreme Court found it to be in violation of the Sherman Antitrust Act. Americans smoked just over ten billion cigarettes that year.

28   Four companies emerged from the old trust: a smaller American, Liggett & Myers, Lorillard, and R. J. Reynolds. With Philip Morris and Brown & Williamson, these companies continue to dominate an industry that last year poured out 704 billion cigarettes, of which 90 percent were smoked in the United States by some 54 million adults and five million adolescents.

29   The cigarette century is clearly at an end. Smoking a cigarette will never again be regarded as altogether normal behavior. But it is much too early to announce the demise of an industry that brought in $17 billion last year.

William Bennett, M.D., is associate editor of the Harvard Medical School Health Letter.

—Reprinted by permission from the September/October issue of *Science 80* magazine. © 1980 by The American Association for the Advancement of Science.

Postreading

TRUE OR FALSE

Directions: Decide if each of the following statements is true (T) or false (F) based on the selection.

_____ **1.** Allen and Ginter invented the first cigarette-rolling machine.

_____ **2.** The Europeans, who brought tobacco to this country, developed a better-tasting and milder tobacco.

_____ **3.** By changing their method of curing, tobacco growers developed a more addicting tobacco.

_____ **4.** Because cigarette smoke is absorbed into the bloodstream at a slow rate, it becomes very addicting.

_____ **5.** It appears that cigarettes are more psychologically than physiologically addicting.

_____ **6.** To heavy smokers, avoiding the unpleasantness of withdrawal symptoms is a major reason for continuing smoking.

_____ **7.** Cigarette smokers generally are more relaxed than nonsmokers due to the calming effect of nicotine.

_____ **8.** Because urine is slightly acid in the morning, smokers often want to smoke at this time.

_____ **9.** The lower the level of nicotine falls, the more likely a person will want to smoke.

_____ **10.** Nicotine becomes highly addictive only when it is inhaled.

READING WORKSHEET

Directions: After you have completed the true-or-false exercise, answer the following questions. You may refer to the selection if necessary.

1. The selection begins with a list of well-known names. Why has the author chosen these names? _____

_____

Why do you think the author begins the article in this way? _____

_____

2. In paragraph 5, the phrase *a kind of dandified luxury* is set off by dashes (—). Why? _____

_____

3. In paragraph 6, what invention is the author referring to when he states "the invention?" _____

_____

4. What does *a waning vice* refer to in paragraph 8? _____

_____

5. Which of the following questions sums up the first question asked in paragraph 8?
   a. Why did the demand for cigarettes increase?
   b. Why did people smoke?
   c. Why were tobacco growers poor?

6. Write a question that paraphrases the second question asked in paragraph 8. _____

_____

7. Why is tobacco compared with dried cabbage? How do they differ?

_____

_____

8. What is the opposite of acid? What word in paragraph 13, signals this contrast? _____

_____

9. Why are the tobacco-growing parts of Virginia and North Carolina referred to as the *Old Bright Belt*?

_____

_____

10. The author makes a comparison between the time it takes nicotine to reach the brain and the time it takes heroin to reach the brain. Fill in the blanks below with the correct information from the text.

Nicotine:
a. percentage of nicotine that reaches the brain = _____

b. speed = _____

Heroin:
a. percentage of heroin that reaches the brain = _____

b. speed = _____

Which drug is more potent? _____

This kind of comparison is called an analogy. Analogies add strength to arguments. How is strength added in this situation?

_____

11. The author could have compared nicotine to sugar, another substance absorbed quickly into the bloodstream. Why did the author choose heroin instead of another substance such as sugar? _____

_____

12. Other analogies are used in this article. A child's pacifier and security blanket are compared to _____.
What is the purpose of this comparison? _____

_____

13. In paragraph 17, we read "for about a fifth." A fifth of who/what?

_____

14. According to paragraph 18, what can be said about most addictive substances but not cigarettes? _____

_____

15. In paragraph 19, we read "First, they give an ill-defined. . . . "
What does *they* refer to? _____

_____

16. According to paragraph 22, why do people smoke? _____

_____

17. The semicolons (;) in paragraph 23 are used to show
   a. additional information.
   b. cause and result.
   c. chronological order.

18. Many people who try to stop smoking cigarettes find themselves eating more. Why would this be detrimental to their effort to quit smoking?

_____

_____

19. We read that smokers avoid smoking in the morning because of the side effects. What side effects is the author referring to? _____

_____

20. What discovery did James Buchanan Duke make? _____

_____

21. Duke's discovery described in paragraph 26 gives added information to a previous paragraph discussing curing methods. What is the number of this previous paragraph? _____

22. In paragraph 25, we read "He leased . . . " Locate this sentence. Commas in this sentence are used to show
   a. contrast.
   b. a restatement of ideas.
   c. chronological order.

23. Why does the author say that "the cigarette century is clearly at an end"? What information can be used to support this opinion?

_____

_____

_____

_____

24. Many authors reveal their opinion in their writing. They are subjective, in other words. Is the author of this selection subjective or objective (offering little or no opinion)? Give examples from the selection to support your opinion. _____

_____

_____

25. Number the following list of events to indicate what happened first, second, and so on.

_____ Society began to frown on smoking.

_____ Many people became addicted to cigarettes.

_____ Cigarettes were rolled by hand.

_____ The method of tobacco production changed.

_____ James Bonsack invented a machine for rolling cigarettes.

_____ The cigarette industry became modernized.

INFERENCE AND RESTATEMENT

Directions: Decide whether each of the following is a restatement (R), an inference (I), or a false statement (F) according to the selection. If the sentence is a restatement, locate the original in the selection and give the paragraph number where it is found.

_____ **1.** There were no cigarette-producing machines prior to 1880.

_____ **2.** Although most people are aware of the dangers of cigarette smoking, very few desire to stop.

_____ **3.** *Nicotiana* is a type of tobacco.

_____ **4.** The "Old Bright Belt" received its name because of the technique involved in heating tobacco.

_____ **5.** A large amount of nicotine is absorbed in the mouth before it gets to the lungs.

_____ **6.** Nicotine does not pass through living tissue when it is in an acid medium.

_____ **7.** Smoking cigarettes does not calm down a person but instead helps prevent that person from becoming further annoyed.

_____ **8.** Many smokers light up a cigarette after meals.

_____ **9.** Cigarettes remain in high demand due to their addictive quality.

_____**10.** The tobacco industry was unaware that the change in curing methods made a remarkable difference in the composition of cigarettes.

VOCABULARY FROM CONTEXT

Directions: *Using your own knowledge and information from the text, answer the following questions. Refer to the selection while you work. Don't be afraid to guess.*

1. in retrospect (paragraph 8)
In this paragraph, the author discusses events from the past related to the fall in cigarette consumption.

In retrospect means _____.

2. opprobrium (paragraph 8)
In this sentence, cigarette smoking is labeled a vice. With that attitude toward smoking, you can guess that

Opprobrium means _____.

3. impoverished (paragraph 8)
An antonym for this word can be found in the same paragraph.

Impoverished means _____.

4. physiological (paragraph 17)
Physiological need is contrasted with psychological need.

Physiological means _____.

5. paradox (paragraph 24)
In this paragraph, the author presents the paradox, then explains it.

Paradox means_____.

6. demise (paragraph 29)
In this paragraph, the author states that the cigarette century is at an end.

Demise means _____.

SKILLS CHECKUP: CHRONOLOGICAL ORGANIZATION

Directions: Below is an incomplete list of the important events and their corresponding dates as discussed in the selection. Complete the list, referring to the text as necessary. Note the date or time period, and any people who may have been involved. Notice that related events are grouped together.

Date or Time Period	Event	Relevant People
1. 1612	A milder tobacco was brought from the Caribbean.	John Rolfe
2. after the American Civil War (in the 19th century)		
3. (a) 1869	All cigarettes were hand-rolled.	
(b) 1875		
(c)	First cigarette-rolling machine, the "Bonsack," was invented.	
4. (a) 1865		
(b)	American Trade Company was founded.	Dukes of Durham
(c) 1911		

SUMMARY

Directions: Fill in the blanks so that the following summary is logical, grammatically correct, and accurate according to the selection.

There were two events in the history of the cigarette _____ that greatly changed the smoking _____ of people during the last _____.

The first of these _____ was the invention of a _____ by _____ that rolled and cut cigarettes precisely and quickly. Bonsack's machine made it possible for more _____ to get into the hands of more smokers.

The second and more important of these _____ was a change in the method of _____ tobacco. The first _____ produced in the Old Bright Belt was not mild enough to be _____. After tobacco producers began to _____ the tobacco over open fires during processing, the smoke that resulted became mild enough to inhale. After this, producers of tobacco began to cure the tobacco using flues. The effect of this _____ was significant in that the _____ delivered from flue-cured _____ was slightly _____ and therefore more addictive.

As more of the population became _____, the demand for cigarettes _____ and, within 75 years, the cigarette _____ had grown into a major business concern.

But, now, with more and more convincing evidence about the dangers of _____ appearing every day, _____ is losing its popularity. It is no longer considered a completely _____activity.

ESSAY QUESTIONS

Directions: In one to three paragraphs, answer the following questions using information from the selection to support your ideas.

1. Describe the difference between the general chemical makeup of heat-cured and air-cured tobacco and explain how this difference relates to cigarette addiction.

2. Compare the concepts of psychological and physiological addiction. How do these concepts apply to cigarette smoking?

RELATED READING

PAYING THE PIPER

WILLIAM BENNETT

When experiments on animals turn up carcinogens in our favorite foods and everyday consumer items, some critics invariably dismiss the data as coming only from animals. The tobacco industry has, of necessity, taken the opposite tack; for years it has argued that the evidence incriminating cigarettes shows merely a "statistical association" because it comes from studies of human deaths, not animal experiments. By now, though, the evidence that

cigarettes shorten life is overwhelming; the causal connection is as firmly established as any in medicine. "Indeed," writes John Cairns, a molecular biologist and expert on cancer, "in retrospect, it is almost as if Western societies had set out to conduct a vast and fairly well controlled experiment in carcinogenesis, bringing about several million deaths and using their own people as the experimental animals."

But the cancer connection, which was the most obvious and easiest to establish, is not the major cause of death

in smokers. Rather, it is coronary heart disease. Second comes lung cancer. General deterioration of the lung tissue is third. After these three major causes, a variety of other diseases and cancers make a further contribution to the high death rate of smokers. Cancers of the larynx, mouth, esophagus, bladder, kidney, and pancreas are all more common in smokers than nonsmokers. So are ulcers of the stomach and intestine, which are more likely to be fatal in smokers.

Women who smoke during pregnancy run a significant risk that their babies will die before or at birth. The newborns are likely to weigh less, to arrive prematurely, and to be more susceptible to "sudden infant death."

The risk of smoking is, in general, a 70 percent increase in the probability of dying at any age—100 percent for a two-pack smoker. As a rule of thumb, each cigarette knocks about five minutes off the smoker's life. For an average habit, that adds up to six or seven years (more for some, less for others). In the meantime, smokers lose more work days to illness than nonsmokers and spend more time in the hospital.

The ill effects of smoking are mostly, but not entirely,

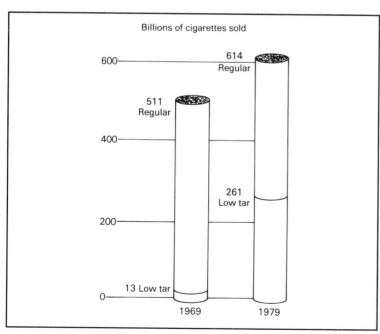

Low tar sales have soared in a decade.

a consequence of the amount of inhaled smoke. Virtually all cigarette smokers inhale, even those who say they do not, and they continue to do so when they switch to pipe or cigars.

Cigarette smoke is loaded with poisions and carcinogens. The "tars," particles of organic matter, are largely responsible for causing cancer, or, perhaps, for promoting the growth of tumors started by other agents. Nicotine and carbon monoxide are thought to be the main cause of heart disease; there is debate about their relative importance.

In response to public worry about the health hazards of smoking, cigarette manufacturers over the last decade have progressively lowered the tar and nicotine content. These "lighter" brands appear to be effeicive in reducing rates of lung cancer. There may be a similar effect for heart disease, but the evidence is not as good. Smokers of low-tar cigarettes appear to get no protection from other respiratory illnesses.

In order to elicit recommendations for his 1981 report on smoking, Surgeon General Julius B. Richmond . . . called a conference to set research priorities for low-tar cigarettes. One area of concern was quickly established: The light cigarettes

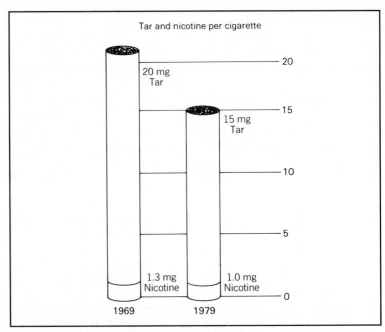

Tar and nicotine per cigarette

20 mg Tar — 20

15 mg Tar — 15

— 10

— 5

1.3 mg Nicotine   1.0 mg Nicotine — 0

1969   1979

Tar and nicotine content has dropped.

may pose a risk for pregnant women. Dr. Jesse Steinfeld, dean of the Medical College of Virginia in Richmond, speculates that the villain in low-tars may be carbon monoxide, since it "binds hemoglobin and may restrict the oxygen a baby needs from the mother's blood."

Carbon monoxide may turn out to be harmful to adults as well. In fact, questions abound on the safety of light cigarettes. We still do not know whether smokers who switch to low-tar cigarettes smoke more and inhale more deeply. If they do, those smokers are at least partly offsetting the presumed advantage of switching. Another question concerns whether the availability of these "safer" cigarettes has encouraged a large number of young people who otherwise would not have smoked to begin the habit. All in all, we are still far from knowing whether the low-tar, low-nicotine cigarettes will ultimately prove to be a Good Thing.

—Reprinted by permission from the September/October issue of *Science 80* magazine. © 1980 by The American Association for the Advancement of Science. (Excerpted from article on pp. 120–126.)

DISCUSSION

Read the following questions. Be prepared to discuss them.

1. Currently, cigarette smoking is limited to certain areas in public places, and banned entirely in others. Do you believe that cigarette smoking should be entirely prohibited in public places?

2. Manufacturers generally are held responsible for any hazard presented by their products. For example, if a manufacturer knows that product is dangerous he may be liable for any harm caused by the product. Should cigarette makers also be held responsible for the effects that their products have on the public?

3. Do you believe that a government has the right to tell people if and where they can smoke?

7

From the Old World to the New

Prereading

DISCUSSION

Directions: Read the following questions. Be prepared to discuss them.

1. What are some reasons that people emigrate to other countries?

2. Look up the word *colony* in a dictionary. What does *colony* mean? What does it mean to colonize?

3. This selection describes the first English attempts to colonize America. Why do you think England and other countries wanted to establish settlements in America?

4. In which part of the country is New England? Why do you think that this part of the country is called *New England*?

5. Discuss some of the problems that new settlers might have had in colonizing America.

6. Who is paying for your education in the United States? If you are sponsored, why does your sponsor wish to finance your education? How might your sponsor profit?

PREVIEW

Directions: Read the title and any subheadings of the selection. Also look at the illustrations and read any captions. Then, without reading the selection, answer the following questions.

1. How is this unit organized?
   a. comparison and contrast
   b. chronological order
   c. cause and effect

2. Which two early settlements are described here? _____

3. In which type of text would this unit be found? _____

4. What place names can you locate in this selection? (Identify cities, areas, and countries if possible.) _____

_____

5. Locate names of people within the selection. From looking at the information immediately before and after each name, write down anything that you may have learned about these people.
Example:
a. Queen Elizabeth: "Virgin Queen"; Queen of England; late sixteenth century; granted money for expeditions to America.

b. _____

c. _____

d. _____

e. _____

READING

FROM THE OLD WORLD TO THE NEW

The First English Settlements

1   The first English attempts to colonize the New World were sporadic, private efforts. There was little planning or direction from the government; instead, the early colonies resulted from the array of economic and social pressures that had been building in England through much of the late sixteenth century. Those

Source: From *American History: A Survey,* Sixth Edition, by Richard N. Current, T. Harry Williams, Frank Freidel, and Alan Brinkley. Copyright © 1959, 1961, 1964, 1966, 1971, 1975, 1979 by Richard N. Current, T. Harry Williams, and Frank Freidel. Copyright © 1983 by Richard N. Current, T. Harry Williams, Frank Freidel, and Alan Brinkley. Reprinted by permission of Alfred A. Knopf, Inc.

pressures not only encouraged the development of colonies; they also helped determine what those colonies would be like.

2   Three conditions in particular shaped the character of the first English settlements. First, the colonies were business enterprises. They were financed and directed by private companies, to which the colonists were directly responsible. However much the early settlers might have dreamed of a better life in the New World, therefore, one of their first concerns was to produce a profit for their corporate sponsors. Second, because the colonies were tied only indirectly to the Crown (which char-

SIR WALTER RALEIGH *Raleigh was a prominent figure in many aspects of the life of Elizabethan England. He served in the British military effort in Ireland in the 1570s, became a popular and influential favorite in the court of Queen Elizabeth in the 1580s, and served in Parliament in the 1590s—before finally falling into the disgrace that would ultimately lead to his execution in 1618. And Raleigh was also important as one of the major forces behind early English efforts to explore and colonize the New World. (Library of Congress)*

tered the private companies but took little interest in them thereafter), they would from the start begin to develop their own political and social institutions. And third, the English colonies, unlike those of the Spanish to the south, would be "transplantations" of societies from the Old World to the New. (Hence the term "plantation," which was used to describe most of the first settlements.) There would be no effort to blend

European society with the society of the natives, as there was in many of the Spanish colonies. The English would, as far as they could, isolate themselves from the Indians and create enclosed societies that would be entirely their own.

Early Attempts

3   The pioneers of English colonization were Sir Humphrey Gilbert and his half-brother Sir Walter Raleigh, though neither of them succeeded in founding a permanent colony. Both were friends of Queen Elizabeth. While Drake and other "sea dogs" were harrying the Spaniards in the New World and on the seas, Gilbert kept insisting at court that English bases in America would give still greater opportunities for sapping the power of Spain. In 1578, he obtained from Elizabeth a patent granting him, for six years, the exclusive right "to inhabit and possess at his choice all remote and heathen lands not in the actual possession of any Christian prince."

4   That same year, Gilbert and Raleigh, with seven ships and nearly 400 men, set out to establish a base in the New World. Storms turned them back before they had crossed the ocean. Gilbert waited five years while he sought to raise enough money to try again. Then, in 1583, he sailed with a second and smaller expedition, reached Newfoundland, and took possession of it in the queen's name. He proceeded southward along the coast, looking for a good place to build a military outpost that might eventually grow into a profitable colony, of which he would be proprietor. Once more a storm defeated him; this time his ship sank, and he was lost at sea.

5   The next year, Raleigh, securing from Elizabeth a six-year grant similar to Gilbert's, sent out men to look over the American coast. They returned with two Indians and with glowing reports of an island the natives called Roanoke, and of its environs (in what is now North Carolina). With her permission Raleigh named the area "Virginia" in honor of Elizabeth, the "Virgin Queen." He expected financial aid in return but she said she could not afford it. So he had to raise money from private investors to finance another voyage to Roanoke. The hundred men he sent out in 1585 spent a year in America, exploring as far north as the Chesapeake Bay, which they recommended as the best location for a settlement.

6   In 1587, Raleigh sponsored still another expedition, this one carrying ninety-one men, seventeen women (two of them pregnant), and nine children as colonists. He directed them to the Chesapeake Bay, but the pilot nevertheless landed them on Roanoke Island. Here one of the women gave birth to Virginia Dare, the first American-born child of English parents. A relief ship, delayed until 1590 by the hostilities with Spain, found the island utterly deserted. What had become of the "lost colony" is still a mystery.

7   The colonizing efforts of Gilbert and Raleigh taught lessons and set examples for later and more successful promoters of colonization. After sending out his ill-fated settlers, Raleigh again sought financial aid from merchants, to whom he sold rights of trading with his proposed colony. He realized that the undertaking was too big for the purse of one man alone. Some of the colonizers after him raised funds for their ventures by forming companies and selling stock, but others, as individuals or unincorporated groups,

THE PORTRAICTVER OF CAPTAYNE IOHN SMITH ADMIRALL OF NEW ENGLAND.

Æta 37.
A° 1616.

These are the Lines that shew thy Face: but those
That shew thy Grace and Glory brighter bee:
Thy Faire-Discoueries and Fowle - Overthrowes
Of Salvages, much Civilliz'd by thee
Best shew thy Spirit, and to it Glory Wyn:
So, thou art Brasse without, but Golde within.
If so, in Brasse, too soft smiths Acts to beare)
I fix thy Fame, to make Brasse steele out weare.

Thine as thou art Virtues.
John Davies Heref.

CAPTAIN JOHN SMITH *Long before John Smith gained fame as the leader and, as many believe, the savior of the English settlement at Jamestown, Virginia, he had engaged in numerous foreign escapades as a roving adventurer. According to his own immodest accounts, he spent years in eastern Europe fighting in wars against the Turks and was even a slave in Turkey for a time. After returning to England from Virginia in 1609, Smith made at least one additional journey to North America, visiting New England on behalf of a group of London merchants in 1614. In his later years, he wrote numerous books about his experiences, the last of which he completed in 1631, the year of his death. (Library of Congress)*

continued to depend on their own resources.

8   After the accession of James I, Raleigh was accused of plotting against the king, deprived of his monopoly, imprisoned, and eventually executed. None of his successors received grants so vast and undefined as both his and Gilbert's had been. Thereafter the Crown, in theory the owner as well as the sovereign of lands to be occupied by Englishmen, granted and regranted territory to companies or proprietors, on terms that imposed varying conditions and set boundaries that often were conflicting and vague.

9   A group of London merchants, to whom Raleigh had assigned his charter rights, planned to renew his attempts at colonization in Virginia, which still consisted of an undefined stretch along the Atlantic seaboard. A rival group of merchants, who lived in Plymouth and other West Country towns, were also interested in American ventures. They were already sponsoring voyages of exploration to the coast farther north, up to Newfoundland, where West Country fishermen had been going for many years.

10   In 1606, James I issued a new charter, which divided America between the two groups. The London Company got the exclusive right to colonize in the south (between the 34th and the 41st parallels), and the Plymouth Company the same right in the north (between the 38th and the 45th parallels). These areas overlapped, but neither company was allowed to start a colony within a hundred miles of the other. Each company, as soon as it had begun actual colonization, was to receive a grant of land a hundred miles wide and a hundred miles deep. The settlers themselves were to retain all the "liberties, franchises, and immu-nities" that belonged to Englishmen at home.

11   Through the efforts of the London Company (or Virginia Company of London, its full name), the first enduring English colony was about to be planted in America. The merchants, taking the East India Company as their model, intended at the outset to found not an agricultural settlement but a trading post. To it they expected to send English manufactures for barter with the Indians, and from it they hoped to bring back American commodities procured in exchange or produced by the labor of their own employees.

Jamestown

12   The first English settlers on the North American continent arrived in the spring of 1607. They were the 100 men (the survivors of a group of 144 who had embarked from England) of the London Company's first expedition; and their three ships (the *Godspeed*, the *Discovery*, and the *Susan Constant*) sailed into the Chesapeake Bay and up the James River, on whose banks they established their colony.

13   They chose their site poorly. Under instructions from the company to avoid the mistakes of Roanoke (whose residents were assumed to have been murdered by Indians) and select an easily defended location, they chose an inland setting that they believed would offer them security. But the site was low and swampy, intolerably hot and humid in the summer and prey to outbreaks of malaria. It was surrounded by thick woods, which were hard to clear for cultivation. And it was soon threatened by hostile Indians of a confederation led by the imperial chief Powhatan.

14   The result could hardly have been

more disastrous. For seventeen years, one after another wave of settlers attempted to make Jamestown a habitable and profitable colony. Every effort failed. The town became instead a place of misery and death; and the London Company, which had sponsored it in the hope of vast profits, saw itself drained of funds and saddled with endless losses. All that could be said of Jamestown at the end of this first period of its existence was that it had survived.

15 The colonists, too many of whom were adventurous gentlemen and too few of whom were willing laborers, ran into serious difficulties from the moment they landed. They faced an overwhelming task in trying to sustain themselves, and the promoters in London complicated the task by demanding a quick return on their investment. When the men in Jamestown ought to have been growing food, they were required to hunt for gold and to pile up lumber, tar, pitch, and iron ore for export. By January 1608, when ships appeared with additional men and supplies, all but thirty-eight of the first arrivals were dead.

16 Jamestown, already facing extinction, was carried through the crisis mainly by the efforts of twenty-seven-year-old Captain John Smith, hero of his own narratives of hairbreadth escapes from both Turks and Indians but a sensible and capable man. Leadership in the colony had been divided among the several members of a council who quarreled continually until Smith, as council president, asserted his will. He imposed work and order on the community. During the next winter, fewer than a dozen (in a population of about 200) succumbed. By the summer of 1609, when Smith was deposed from the council and returned to England for the treatment of a serious powder burn, the colony was showing promise of survival, though in fact its worst trials were yet to come.

17 Already the promoters in London were making a strenuous effort to build up the Virginia colony. To raise money and men, they sold company stock to "adventurers" planning to remain at home, gave shares to "planters" willing to migrate at their own expense, and provided passage for poor men agreeing to serve the company for seven years. Under a new communal plan, the company would hold all land and carry on all trade for a seven-year period. The settlers would contribute their labor to the common enterprise and draw upon a company storehouse for their subsistence. At the end of the period, the profits would be divided among the stockholders. The London merchants obtained a new charter (1609), which increased their power over the colony and enlarged its area (to a width of 400 miles north and south and a length extending all the way "from sea to sea, west and northwest"). In the spring of 1609, the company sent off to Virginia a "great fleet" of nine vessels with about 600 men, women, and children aboard.

18 Disaster followed. One of the Virginia-bound ships sank in a hurricane, and another ran aground on one of the Bermuda islands. Many of those who reached Jamestown, still weak from their long and stormy voyage, succumbed to fevers before winter came. That winter of 1609–1610 turned into a "starving time" worse than anything before. While Indians killed off the livestock in the woods and kept the settlers within the palisade, these unfortunates were reduced to eating "dogs, cats, rats, snakes, toadstools, horsehides," and even the "corpses of dead men," as one survivor recalled. When the

INDIAN ATTACK ON VIRGINIA *The arduous early years of white settlement in Virginia were marked not only by the demoralization and apparent indolence of the settlers, but by periodic conflict with hostile Indian tribes. This 1662 illustration of an Indian attack on a Virginia community suggests the terror with which whites viewed the native threat. Whites are depicted here as virtually helpless, while half-naked "savages" slaughter men, women, and children indiscriminately. War canoes filled with still more Indians can be seen heading toward shore in the background, reflecting the whites' awareness that—in the mid-seventeenth century, at least—they were still greatly outnumbered. (Library of Congress)*

migrants who had been stranded on Bermuda arrived at Jamestown the following May, they found about 60 scarcely human wretches still alive (there had been nearly 500 people there the previous summer). No one could see much point in staying, and soon all were on their way downriver, leaving the town to its decay.

19 Yet the colony was to begin again. The refugees met a relief ship coming up the river and were persuaded to go back to Jamestown. This ship was part of a fleet bringing supplies and the colony's first governor, Lord De La Warr. He reestablished the settlement and imposed strict discipline, then went home because of illness, while new relief expeditions with hundreds of colonists began to arrive. De La Warr's successors Thomas Dale and Thomas Gates continued his harsh rule, sentencing offenders to be flogged, hanged, or broken on the wheel. Under Dale and Gates the colony spread, with new settlements lining the river above and below Jamestown. The communal system of labor was not functioning very well, for despite the governors' strictness the lazy often evaded work, "presuming that howsoever the harvest prospered, the general store must maintain them." Before the seven years of the system were up, Dale changed it to allow the private ownership and cultivation of land in return for part-time work for the company and contributions of grain to its storehouses. Meanwhile the cultivators were discovering, in tobacco, a salable crop.

20 Tobacco had come into use in Europe soon after Columbus's first return from the West Indies, where he had seen the Cuban natives smoking small cigars (*tabacos*), which they inserted in the nostril. In England Sir Walter Raleigh popularized the smoking habit, and the demand for tobacco soared despite objections on both hygenic and economic grounds. Some critics denounced it as a poisonous weed, the cause of many diseases. King James I himself led the attack with *A Counterblaste to Tobacco* (1604), in which he urged his people not to imitate "the barbarous and beastly manners of the wild, godless, and slavish Indians, especially in so vile and stinking a custom." Other critics were concerned because England's tobacco imports came from the Spanish colonies and resulted in the loss of English gold. In 1612, the Jamestown planter John Rolfe began to experiment with the West Indian plant. It grew well in Virginia soil and, though rated less desirable than the Spanish-grown, found ready buyers in England. Tobacco cultivation quickly spread up and down the James.

21 When the seven-year communal period was up (1616), the company had no profits to divide, but only land and debts. Still, the promoters were generally optimistic because of their success with tobacco. In 1618, they launched a last great campaign to attract settlers and make the colony profitable. They offered a "headright" of fifty acres to anyone who paid his own or someone else's passage to Virginia, and another fifty for each additional migrant whose way he paid. Thus a wealthy man could send or take servants to work for him and receive, in return, a sizable plantation. The company expected to add to its income by charging the headright landholder a small quitrent (one shilling a year for every fifty acres). Old investors and settlers were given grants of one hundred acres apiece. To make life in the colony more attractive, the company promised the colonists the rights of Englishmen (as provided in the original charter of 1606), an end to the

strict and arbitrary rule, and even a share in self-government. To diversify the colonial economy, the company undertook to transport iron-workers and other skilled craftsmen to Virginia.

22   On July 30, 1619, in the James-town church, delegates from the various communities met as the House of Burgesses to consider, along with the governor and his council, the enactment of laws for the colony. This was a major portent of the future—the first meeting of an elected legislature, a representative assembly, within what was to become the United States. A month later, there occurred in Virginia another event with a less happy outcome. As John Rolfe recorded, "about the latter end of August" a Dutch ship brought in "20 and odd Negroes." These black persons were brought, it seems, not as slaves but as servants to be held for a term of years and then freed, like the white servants with whom the planters already were familiar. But whether or not anyone realized it at the time, a start had been made toward the enslavement of Africans within what was to be the American republic.

23   For several years the Indians had given the Virginia colonists little trouble. A kind of truce had resulted from the capture of the great chief Powhatan's daughter Pocahontas and her marriage (1614) to John Rolfe. Going with her husband on a visit to England, Pocahontas as a Christian convert and a gracious woman stir-red up interest in projects to civilize the Indians. She died while abroad. Then Powhatan also died, and his brother Opechancanough replaced him as head of the native confed-eracy. Under Opechancanough, the Indians pretended to be friendly while laying plans to eliminate the English intruders. On a March morning in 1622, the tribesmen called on the white settlements as if to offer goods for sale, then suddenly turned to killing and were not stopped until 347 whites of both sexes and all ages, including Rolfe, lay dead or dying. The surviving En-glishmen struck back with merciless revenge and gave up all thought of civilizing the aborigines.

24   The massacre was the final blow to the already staggering London Company, which had poured virtu-ally all its funds into its profitless company and now faced imminent bankruptcy. In 1624, James I re-voked the company's charter; and the colony at last came under the control of the Crown. So it would remain until 1776.

25   The worst of Virginia's troubles were now over. The colony had weathered a series of disasters and had established itself as a permanent settlement. It had developed a cash crop that promised at least modest profits. It had established a rudimen-tary representative government. And it could now realistically hope for future growth and prosperity. But these successes had come at a high cost. By 1624, the white population of Virginia stood at 1,300. In the preceding seventeen years, more than 8,500 white settlers had arrived in the colony. Over 80 percent of them, in other words, had died.

Plymouth Plantation

26   While the London Company was starting the colonization of James-town, the Plymouth Company at-tempted to found a colony far to the north, at the mouth of the Kennebec River (on the coast of what is now Maine). But in a year the surviving colonists returned to England. The Plymouth Colony made no further attempts to colonize. The most it did

was to send Captain John Smith, after his return from Jamestown, to look over its territory. He drew a map of the area, wrote an enthusiastic pamphlet about it, and named it "New England." Eventually the Plymouth merchants reorganized as the Council for New England and, with a new, sea-to-sea land grant from the king, proceeded to deal in real estate on a tremendous scale.

27   The first enduring settlement in New England—the second in English America—resulted from the discontent of a congregation of Puritan Separatists. From time to time Separatists had been imprisoned and even executed for persisting in their defiance of the government and the Church of England. A band of them in the hamlet of Scrooby looked to Holland as a country where they might worship as they pleased, though it was against the law to leave the realm without the king's consent. Slipping away a few at a time, members of the Scrooby congregation crossed the English Channel and began their lives anew in Holland. Here they were allowed to meet and hold their services without interference. But, as aliens, they were not allowed to join the Dutch guilds of craftsmen, and so they had to work long and hard at unskilled and poorly paid jobs. They were further troubled as their children began to speak Dutch, marry into Dutch families, and lose their Englishness. Some of the Puritans decided to move again, this time across the Atlantic, where they might find opportunity for happier living and also for spreading "the gospel of the Kingdom of Christ in those remote parts of the world."

28   Leaders of this group got permission from the London Company to settle as an independent community with land of its own in Virginia. They tried, and failed, to get from James I a guarantee of religious freedom, but they were assured that he would "not molest them, provided they carried themselves peaceably." This was a historic concession on the part of the king, for it opened English America to settlement by dissenting Protestants. The next step was to arrange financing. Several English merchants agreed to advance the necessary funds, on the condition that a communal plan like that of Jamestown be put into effect, with the merchants to share the profits at the end of seven years.

29   The migrating Puritans "knew they were pilgrims" when they left Holland, their leader and historian, William Bradford, later wrote. The sailing from Plymouth was delayed, and it was not until September that the *Mayflower*, with thirty-five "saints" (Puritan Separatists) and sixty-seven "strangers" aboard, finally put out to sea. Their destination was probably the mouth of the Hudson River, in the northeast corner of the London Company's Virginia grant, but when they sighted Cape Cod in November, it was too late in the year to go on. After reconnoitering, they chose a site in an area that John Smith had labeled "Plymouth" on his map. Since this area lay outside the London Company's territory, they would be without a government once ashore, and some of the "strangers" began to show a lawless spirit. One of the "saints" therefore drew up an agreement, which forty-one of the passengers signed. This Mayflower Compact was like the church covenant by which the Separatists formed congregations, except that it set up a civil government, and it professed allegiance to the king. Then, on December 21, 1620, the Pilgrims landed at Plymouth Rock.

30   They settled on cleared land that

The Mayflower Compact [1620]

In the name of God, Amen. We, whose names are underwritten, the Loyal Subjects of our dread Sovereign Lord King James, by the Grace of God, of Great Britain, France, and Ireland, King, Defender of the Faith, & Having undertaken for the Glory of God, and Advancement of the Christian Faith, and the Honour of our King and Country, a Voyage to plant the first colony in the northern Parts of Virginia; Do by these presents, solemnly and mutually in the Presence of God and one another, covenant and combine ourselves together into a civil Body Politick, for our better Ordering and Preservation, and Furtherance of the Ends aforesaid; And by Virtue hereof do enact, constitute, and frame, such just and equal Laws, Ordinances, Acts, Constitutions, and Offices, from time to time, as shall be thought most meet and convenient for the general Good of the Colony; unto which we promise all due Submission and Obedience.

had been an Indian village until, several years earlier, an epidemic had swept the place. During the first winter, half of the colonists perished from scurvy and exposure, but the rest managed to put the colony on its feet. Among the neighboring Indians, whose military power had been weakened by the recent plague, the Pilgrims discovered friends— Squanto, Samoset, Massasoit—who showed them how to obtain seafood and cultivate corn. After the first harvest, the settlers invited the Indians to join them in an October festival, the original Thanksgiving. They could not aspire to rich farms on the sandy and marshy soil, but they soon developed a profitable trade in fish and furs. From time to time new colonists arrived from England, and in a decade the population reached the modest total of 300.

31   The people of "Plymouth Plantation" were entitled to elect their own governor, and they chose the greathearted William Bradford again and again. As early as 1621 he cleared their land title with a patent from the Council for New England, but he never succeeded in his efforts to secure a royal charter giving them indisputable rights of government. Terminating the communal labor plan ahead of schedule, the governor distributed land among the families, thus making "all hands very industrious." He and a group of fellow "undertakers" assumed the colony's debt to its financiers in England and, with earnings from the fur trade, finally paid it off, even though the financiers had not lived up to their agreement to keep on sending supplies.

32   The Pilgrims remained poor; as late as the 1640s they had only one plow among them. Yet they clung to the belief that God had put them in the New World for a reason. Governor Bradford wrote in retrospect: "As one small candle may light a thousand, so the light here kindled hath shone to many, yea, in some sort to our whole nation."

—From *American History: A Survey*, Sixth Edition, by Richard N. Current et al. Knopf, NY, 1979.

Postreading

TRUE OR FALSE

Directions: Decide if each of the following statements is true (T) or false (F) based on the selection.

_____ **1.** The first English colonies were very similar to the Spanish colonies in America.

_____ **2.** Bad weather was Gilbert and Raleigh's worst enemy at the onset of their efforts in colonizing the New World.

_____ **3.** The first area discovered by the English was named *Virginia* after the Queen of England.

_____ **4.** Queen Elizabeth gave financial support to the early pioneers of America when she realized how much money and wealth could be acquired from this "New World."

_____ **5.** The Crown of England exerted complete control over the colonies in America until 1776.

_____ **6.** America was divided into two groups in the early seventeenth century sponsored by the London Company representing England and the Plymouth Company representing Spain.

_____ **7.** Plymouth was settled by the London Company.

_____ **8.** The majority of the first English settlers of Plymouth died because of the poor location of their colony.

_____ **9.** The settlers of Jamestown were forced to be more concerned with making money than growing food.

_____**10.** Because of the good weather, help from the Indians, and the strong motivation of the settlers, the English had a very easy time of colonizing Virginia.

_____**11.** Because of the harsh environment in America, English companies had to give more and more independence and profit to New World settlers in order to keep their business enterprises alive.

_____**12.** While the Jamestown settlers were motivated by business, the colonists of Plymouth were motivated by hopes of religious freedom.

151

READING WORKSHEET

Directions: After you have completed the true-or-false exercise, answer the following questions. You may refer to the selection if necessary.

1. Reread paragraphs 1 and 2. What is the purpose of these paragraphs?

   _____

   _____

2. What are "those pressures" discussed in the first paragraphs?

   a. _____

   b. _____

   What do you think are some examples of these pressures?

   a. _____

   b. _____

3. What are the three conditions that influenced the formation of the colonies (paragraph 2)?

   a. _____

   b. _____

   c. _____

   In your own words, describe how these conditions influenced

   the first English settlements. _____

   _____

   _____

4. How were the English colonies different from the Spanish colonies?

   _____

5. What does *the Crown* refer to in paragraph 2? _____

6. Give some examples of the political and social institutions referred

   to in paragraph 2. _____

   _____

7. Which of the following words signals the same relationship as the word *Hence* in paragraph 2?
   a. Thus
   b. In other words
   c. However

8. What do you think the phrase *at court* means? _____

9. What do you think the term *"sea dogs"* in paragraph 3 means?

   _____ Why is it in quotation marks? _____

10. These "sea dogs" were "harrying" the Spanish in the New World and on the seas. Think about anything you already may know about the relationship between England and Spain during the rule of Elizabeth I. What do you think *harrying* means? _____

11. What do you believe were Sir Humphrey Gilbert's motives in attempting to colonize the New World? _____

    _____

12. What states did the Virginia of the sixteenth century include? (You must refer to more than one paragraph to find the answer.) _____

    _____

13. What do the authors mean when they say that Sir Walter Raleigh "expected financial aid in return" in paragraph 5?
    a. He expected to be paid when he returned.
    b. He expected the Queen to give him money because he named a new land after her.
    c. He expected the Queen to come back to the New World with him.

14. What was the name of the "lost colony"? _____
    Why is it called *lost*? _____

15. What was the name of the London Company's first settlement?

    _____

    Why do you think this name was chosen? _____

16. What were some of the problems facing the settlers of Jamestown? _____

17. Who was Captain John Smith? _____
_____

18. What was the communal plan used in Jamestown? Why do you think that it wasn't successful? _____
_____

19. What is a "headright"? Locate the definition of this term in paragraph 21. _____

20. What was the important "cash crop" developed by Jamestown? _____

21. What was significant about the meeting which occured in Jamestown in July 1619? _____
_____

22. What group settled Plymouth? What were their reasons for wanting to settle in the New World?
_____
_____

23. Who are the "saints" and the "strangers" mentioned in paragraph 29? _____

24. What is the Mayflower Compact? _____
_____

25. Read the closing quote (paragraph 32). What was Governor Bradford saying about the colonial experience at Plymouth? _____
_____
_____

INFERENCE AND RESTATEMENT

Directions: Decide whether each of the following is a restatement (R), and inference (I), or a false statement (F) according to the selection. If the sentence is a restatement, locate the original in the selection and give the paragraph number where it is found.

_____ **1.** Although the English colonists may have come to America in search of more personal freedom or for the chance to improve their standards of living, one of their principle objectives was to make money for the businesses they represented.

_____ **2.** The Spanish sought to mix with the other races that they encountered in the New World rather than maintain pure Spanish societies.

_____ **3.** Sir Walter Raleigh was disappointed when Queen Elizabeth said that she could no longer afford to support his adventures.

_____ **4.** New settlers learned very little from the mistakes of their predecessors.

_____ **5.** After James I became king, Raleigh became unpopular at court, was put in jail, and eventually was executed.

_____ **6.** After Raleigh's death, the king became the owner of all companies set up in the New World, as well as the owner of all of the lands settled.

_____ **7.** The London Company was determined not to allow the Jamestown colony to fail.

_____ **8.** Because of the harsh conditions, the only way to ensure the survival of Jamestown was to enforce strict work rules.

_____ **9.** The Plymouth Company attempted to establish a colony in the North, but all of the colonists died.

_____**10.** The Mayflower Compact provided for a civil government to be set up in the new colony.

OUTLINING

Directions: On the next page is an outline of important dates and their corresponding events. As you fill in the outline, remember to include all relevant information answering who?, where?, what?, and why?

I. Early attempts to colonize the New World by _____

_____

When? <u>Late sixteenth and early seventeenth century</u>

A. First attempts by Gilbert

    1. 1578 expedition

        a) Financing from? _____

        b) Where? _____

        c) Results? _____

    2. 1853 expedition

        a) Where? _____

        b) Results? _____

B. Next attempts by _____

    1. _____

        a) Financing from? <u>Queen Elizabeth,</u>

        b) Where? _____

        c) Results? _____

    2. _____

        a) Financing from? _____

        b) Where? <u>Chesapeake Bay</u>

        c) Results? _____

    3. 1587 expedition

        a) Financing from? _____

        b) Where ? _____

        c) Who? <u>91 men and 17 women</u>

        d) Results? _____

    4. 1590

        a) What? <u>A relief ship</u>

        b) Results? _____

C. Further attempts by _____

    1. 1606

        a) What? American prospects were divided between two businesses:

           (1) _____

           (2) _____

II. Jamestown (sponsored by the _____Company)

    A. Original charter (1606)

        1. 1607 expedition

           a) Who? _____

           b) Financing? _____

           c) Purpose? _____

           d) Result? _____

        2. 1608

Continue outlining all relevant information.

_____

_____

_____

        3. 1609

_____

_____

_____

    B. New charter (1609)

    Purpose? _____

    Changes? _____

        1. 1609 expedition

_____

_____

2. 1616

_____

_____

C. New business efforts (_____)

Purpose? _____

Changes? _____

1. 1619

_____

_____

_____

2. 1622

_____

_____

_____

3. 1624–1776

_____

_____

III. Plymouth Plantation (sponsored by the _____ Company)

A. First expedition

1. Early _____ century (around 16 ____)

a) Where? _____

b) Result? _____

B. Second expedition

1. _____

a) Who? _____

b) Why? _____

c) Where? _____

d) Financing from? _____

2. _____

_____

_____

_____

VOCUBALARY FROM CONTEXT

Directions: Using your own knowledge and information from the text, answer the following questions. Refer to the selection while you work. Don't be afraid to guess.

1. sporadic (paragraph 1)
Read the sentence following the one containing this word. Copy

the phrase that gives you a clue to its meaning. _____

Sporadic means _____.

2. environs (paragraph 5)
Think of related forms of this word that you are familiar with. Is

this a verb, noun, adverb, or adjective? _____

Environs means _____.

3. succumbed (paragraph 16)
The clue to the meaning of this word lies in the general topic of

this and the previous paragraphs. The topic is _____.

Succumbed means _____.

4. aborigines (paragraph 23)
Consider the theme of this paragraph and that the word is a noun.

Aborigines means _____.

5. massacre (paragraph 24)
Even if you don't know the meaning of this word, you know what
it refers to and that it was "the final blow" to the colony.

Massacre means _____.

6. guilds (paragraph 27)

What does the verb *join* tell you about this word? _____

_____

What modern organizations help workers get better pay and work-

ing conditions? _____

Guild means _____.

SUMMARY

Directions: Write a summary about Jamestown based on information in the selection. Include as many of the following words and phrases (or their related forms) as you wish. Begin with this sentence: Jamestown, the first British colony to become successfully established in the New World, met with many difficulties in its first seventeen years.

the London Company	weather conditions
tobacco	illness
Indians	Powhatan
massacre	Pocahontas
John Smith	John Rolfe

ESSAY QUESTIONS

Directions: In one to three paragraphs, answer the following questions using information from the selection to support your ideas.

1. Compare the relationship of the British colonists with the Indians with that of the Spanish colonists to the Indians. What difference in attitude is clear? How do you think this difference in attitude may have affected the way in which the colonies developed?

2. What difference in motivation can be seen between the colonists of Jamestown and those of Plymouth? What effects might this difference have had on the length of time required to establish themselves as permanent colonies?

RELATED READING

'I WAS BORN 1,000 YEARS AGO'

This letter from Dan George, chief of the Capilano Indians of British Columbia, Canada, was read at a symposium on the economic development of the Arctic and the future of Eskimo societies, by Father André-Pierre Steinmann, of Puvirnituq, New Quebec.

OPEN LETTER FROM A CAPILANO INDIAN:

My very good dear friends, I was born a thousand years ago, born in a culture of bows and arrows. But within the span of half a lifetime I was flung across the ages to the culture of the atom bomb.

I was born when people loved nature and spoke to it as though it had a soul: I can remember going up Indian River with my father when I was very young. I can remember him watching the sunlight fires on Mount Pé-Né-Né. I can remember him singing his thanks to it as he often did, singing the Indian words "thanks" very very softly.

And the new people came, more and more people came, like a crushing rushing wave they came, hurling the years aside, and suddenly I found myself a young man in the midst of the twentieth century.

I found myself and my people adrift in this new age but not a part of it, engulfed by its rushing tide but only as a captive eddy going round and round. On little reserves and plots of land, we floated in a kind of grey unreality, ashamed of our culture which you ridiculed, unsure of who we were and where we were going, uncertain of our grip on the present, weak in our hope for the future.

We did not have time to adjust to the startling upheaval around us: we seem to have lost what we had without finding a replacement.

Do you know what it is like to be without moorings? Do you know what it is like to live in surroundings that are ugly? It depresses man, for man must be surrounded by the beautiful if his soul is to grow.

Do you know what it is like to have your race belittled, and have you been made aware of the fact that you are only a burden to the country? Maybe we did not have the skills to make a meaningful contribution, but no one would wait for us to catch up. We were shrugged aside because we were dumb and could never learn.

What is it like to be without pride in your race? Pride in your family? Pride and confidence in yourself?

And now, you hold out your hand and you beckon to me to come over: "Come and integrate," you say, but how can I come? I am naked and ashamed; how can I come in dignity? I have no presents, I have no gifts. What is there in my culture you value? My poor treasure you can only scorn. Am I then to come as a beggar and receive all from your ominpotent hand?

Somehow, I must wait. I must find myself. I must wait until you need something that is me.

Pity I can do without. My manhood, I cannot do without. Can we talk of integration until there is social integration? Until there is integration of hearts and minds you have only a physical presence and the walls are high as the mountain range.

Come with me to the playground of an integrated school. Look, it is recess time, the students pour through the doors. Soon, over there, is a group of white students, and over there, near the fence, a group of native students.

What do we want? We want first of all to be respected and to feel we are people of worth; we want an equal opportunity to succeed in life.

Let no one forget it: we are a people with special

rights guaranteed to us by promises and treaties. We do not beg for these rights, nor do we thank you for them because, God help us, the price we paid was exorbitant. We paid for them with our culture, our dignity and our self-respect.

I know that in your heart you wish you can help. I wonder if there is much you can do, and yet there is a lot you can do. When you meet my children, respect each one for what he is: a child and your brother.

—Chief Dan George, reproduced from *UNESCO Courier* , May/June 1986.

DISCUSSION

After reading the main selection and "I Was Born 1,000 Years Ago," discuss the following questions in class.

1. To whom is this "open letter" written and what do you think was the author's intention?

2. Dan George speaks of a loss of pride and confidence among Indians. What do you think has caused these qualities to be lost?

3. What do you think the author means by the term *integration*? Why do you think integration between Native Americans (Indians) and white Americans (in this reading, the term *American* refers to both Canada and the United States) has been difficult?

4. When one country is colonized by another, certain "rights" are lost by the natives of the colonized country. What rights are often lost with colonization?

5. What do you think are some modern problems that might have directly or indirectly resulted from the conflict of Indian and European cultures during colonization?

6. Can you think of any other group of people in another part of the world that may have had an experience similar to that of Native Americans? How was it similar?

The
Producer

8

Prereading

DISCUSSION

Directions: Read the following questions. Be prepared to discuss them.

1. What are some of the problems facing farmers today?

2. How has farming changed over the last century?

3. What kinds of crops are grown in your native country?

4. Does the government in your native country have any influence over farming?

5. Is farming a profitable occupation in your country?

PREVIEW: PART 1

Directions: Read the title and any subheadings of the selection. Also look at the illustrations and read any captions. Then, without reading the selection, answer the following questions.

1. Look at the title of this selection. What do you think this selection is about?

2. Read the subheading. Answer the following questions:
   a. What do you think Booker T. Whatley's profession is?
   b. What is his strategy?
   c. Considering the title of this article, who do you think "the producer" is?

3. Read paragraph 1. Answer the following questions:
   a. What problems do local farmers have?
   b. What is Whatley's suggestion?

4. Look at the representation of a 30-acre farm on page 169, and read the caption. Answer the following questions:
   a. About how many individual crops are grown on this farm?
   b. Why are time periods given under each crop's name?
   c. Of what value is the pond? the Chinese tallow trees?

5. What do you think is the purpose of this selection? For what kind of audience has this article been written?

PREVIEW: PART 2

Directions: *For each designated section, locate the specified words and phrases, write the number of the paragraph in the space provided, and, using this and your own intuition as a guide, answer the question that follows each item.*

Example: __2__ *"year-round cash flow."*

Why might a year-round cash flow be a new concept for farmers? Usually farmers harvest and sell their crops only once a year.

1. Paragraphs 1 through 8

   a. _____ "professor of horticulture at Tuskegee"

     What do you think Tuskegee is? _____

     _____

     Who was a professor there? _____

   b. _____ "$3,000 per acre"

     What must generate $3,000 per acre? _____

   c. _____ "shelters the farmer"

     From what are farmers sheltered or protected? _____

     _____

   d. _____ "this 25-acre horticultural Eden can be altered"

     Why are changes important to farming? _____

     _____

2. Paragraphs 9 through 19

   a. _____ "'Get big or get out.'"

     Who has presented this idea to farmers? _____

     _____

   b. _____ "the government defined"

     What has the government defined? _____

What is the government's definition? _____

_____

c. _____ "Whatley's definition"

What is Whatley's definition of a small farm? _____

_____

d. _____ "Whatley's common sense"

What is common sense and why do you think it is an important

aspect of farming? _____

_____

3. Paragraphs 20 through 31

    a. _____"the farm grosses over $300,000 a year"

    What is the name of the farm? _____

    b. "Saturday-and-Sunday farmers"

    What do you think this type of farmer is? _____

    _____

    c. "'I see two problems'"

    What are these two problems? _____

    d. *"Five Acres and Independence"*

    What do the words in this title mean to you? _____

    _____

READING

THE PRODUCER

Booker T. Whatley has a novel strategy for the small farmer: Stop thinking soybeans and cotton and start thinking peas, quail, bees, and berries.

BARBARA H. SEEBER

1   In the equipment barn at Tuskegee Institute, Booker T. Whatley, named for Booker T. Washington, the founder of the college, chats with a crew wrestling with a tractor tire. "He's been led down the primrose path," Whatley says, lamenting the plight of a local farmer about to lose his land by foreclosure. "For 40 years he's been planting his 200 acres in cotton and soybeans, and now he's about to go broke. He's got to get out of the big-farmer ball park."

2   "A small farm has got to have high-value crops and a year-round cash flow." A decade ago, after too many years of hearing about failing small farms, Whatley set out to show small farmers how to succeed.

3   Backed by a $250,000 Rockefeller Foundation grant, Whatley, a horticulturist, selected the best-producing fruits and vegetables available, established the right combination of soil and fertilizer for each, and, with a two-man farm crew, planted his crops on 25 acres. Formally, his purpose was to demonstrate that farms as small as that can be efficient, productive, and profitable—grossing well over $100,000 annually within five years. He jokes mildly that he wanted to "turn the green chlorophyll in plants into greenbacks for the farmer."

4   From 1974 until he retired in 1981 as professor of horticulture at Tuskegee, Whatley nurtured his model farm. From that farm arose a formula for a successful small farm.

5   This formula dictates that the farm must provide year-round income from about 10 crops. In the South the harvest would include grapes, sweet potatoes, black-eyed peas, blueberries, strawberries, blackberries, and mustard, collard, and turnip greens. The crops should not compete for harvest labor—strawberries and peaches, for example, don't work together because they ripen simultaneously. Every crop must generate an annual income of at least $3,000 per acre, so such old standbys as lettuce, onions, and white potatoes are out. The crops must be irrigated, and the operation must be full-time, employing a family or about three full-time workers. Most important, the main market for the produce must come from a pick-your-own "club" of 1,000 member households who pay an annual fee of $25 each ($40 if the household buys rights to fish in the farm's pond) and harvest most of the crops. To encourage a large and faithful membership, Whatley stipulates that the farm be on a paved road within 40 miles of a metropolitan area.

6   This plan, culled from the best of modern farming technology and Whatley's observations over a lifetime of farming, shelters the farmer beneath a unique economic umbrella. One or two crops may fail in a given year, but with 10, no one crop accounts for more than a tenth of the yearly income, so losses cannot exceed 10 or 20 percent. The irrigation system guards against drought as well as late spring and early fall frost. And the membership club, unlike other approaches, guarantees a local market. Organic farms, for example, appeal to a clientele that rejects the use of pesticides, and pick-your-own operations cannot count on steady customers.

7   The crops are meticulously chosen for cash flow as well as for variety and yield. Four of the five acres of sweet potatoes grown on a farm in the South, for example, are harvested and cured—a

process of drying and storing to increase shelf life—to provide income through the winter. Every Whatley farm also derives year-round income from a rabbitry, a quail or pheasant rookery, and 60 hives of honeybees that pollinate the crops and provide honey, pollen, and a pollination service. The birds provide meat and eggs. And the rabbits furnish everything but the twitch of their noses: Meat and pelts can be sold to members. Eyes and ears go to pharmaceutical labs. The tail makes luxurious trim for coats. And, says Whatley, "the front feet can be sold to the superstitious and the hind feet for ladies' powder puffs."

8   The crop mix of this 25-acre horticultural Eden can be altered according to climate and customer demand. In the Northeast, for example, Whatley recommends cauliflower, broccoli, Brussels sprouts, and spinach instead of the greens and black-eyed peas he specifies for the South; the lowbush variety of blueberry for the rabbiteye variety that thrives in the South; and sweet corn for sweet potatoes. For the West, Whatley suggests garlic and English walnut, pistachio, and hazelnut trees. In the Midwest, asparagus, beans, and tomatoes replace greens, peas, and sweet potatoes, and highbush blueberries supplant rabbiteye.

9   It amounts to a kind of franchise for the small farm, and Whatley has worked out

the recipe as carefully as Colonel Sanders patented his fried chicken. And with good reason, as he sees it. The U.S. Department of Agriculture, Whatley says, sees small farms simply as scaled-down big farms. He blames decades of small farm failure—some 15 million small farmers have abandoned farming since 1950—on the standard government line. "Get big or get out." While agribusinesses rolled up huge grain and dairy surpluses, the family farm foundered.

10   Twenty-five years ago the government defined small farms as those with total yearly income below $10,000, in effect defining small farms as failures. By the mid-1970s inflation had pushed the income figure to $20,000, still a meager amount for a working farm.

11   Now the government defines a small farm as one with "below median non-metropolitan family income in the state." Whatley's definiton is simpler: "I mean limited acreage. A small farmer is a farmer with 10 to 200 acres of land. I don't mean someone in overalls chewing tobacco and butchering the language."

12   In October 1981 he started *The Small Farm Technical Newsletter,* a kind of *Poor Richard's Almanac* for the small farmer. For $12 a year, the farmer is told when to plant and replant, what yield to expect from each crop, how to prune the grapes, what pesticides to spray and

when, how to manage his membership club. The newsletter has a circulation of about 1,200, which includes two prison inmates. Recently one of them wrote to Whatley: "I tried to operate like the big operator and went bust, and in an effort to save the farm, I entered into a short-term career as a bank robber. . . . I am scheduled for parole this fall and I am most interested in going back to farming."

13   That kind of wide, practical appeal recently prompted a reporter to dub Whatley "the guru of common sense." It's a label that makes him shake his head and chuckle.

14   But it is not only Whatley's common sense that makes him singular. His approach combines homespun solutions with the best of modern technology. To keep bugs down, he recommends the agriculture department's "integrated pest management," which balances natural predators such as ladybugs and praying mantises with fungicides, bactericides, insecticides, and herbicides. The regime Whatley worked out at Tuskegee calls for fungicides such as captan mixed with insecticides such as malathion, parathion, and gouthion—a different mixture each time—and applied sequentially so insects cannot establish resistance.

15   He also suggests a flock of guinea fowl, voracious bug eaters that will reduce the need for pesticides on the strawberries, sweet potatoes, greens, and peas

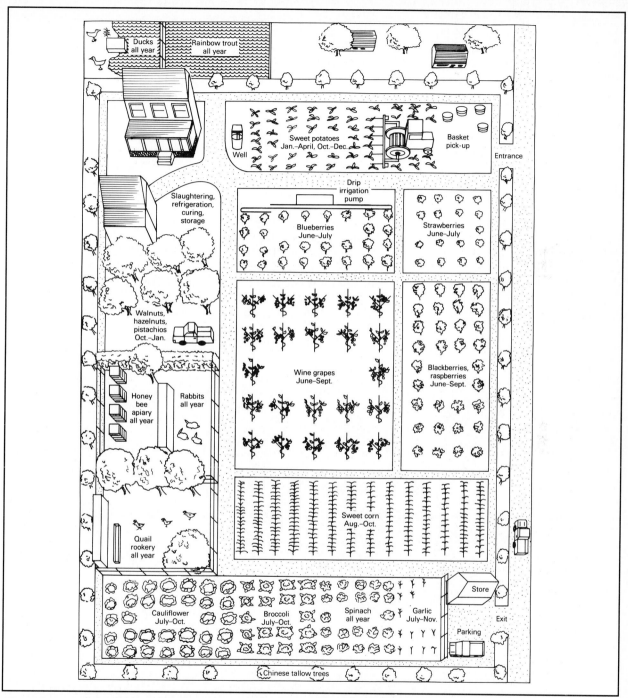

The crop mix of this 30-acre Pacific Northwest farm substitutes caulifower, broccoli, and spinach for Southern greens and corn for black-eyed peas, and adds nut trees and garlic. A five-acre pond 25 feet deep yields up to four tons of rainbow trout; ducks fertilize algae and water plants. The Chinese tallow trees outlining the fields prove irresistible to the bees. (From a drawing by Renee G. Street)

by about 80 percent. To keep deer and rabbits at bay, Whatley strings small bags made from panty hose or cheesecloth, each filled with a fistful of human hair, around his plants. A bag every 20 to 30 feet keeps deer out for as long as 10 months. For rabbits the human hair must be interspersed every eight to 10 feet. "The human smell to deer and rabbits," Whatley chuckles, "is pretty awful." (He gleans the hair from cooperative beauty and barber shops, whose operators have no idea of its purpose. "You can't tell people you're going to string up their hair to keep away the deer and rabbits," he says.)

16   For weed control, Whatley encourages "scratching Mother Nature's back" with a cultivator during the growing season. In addition, he fumigates the seed beds of the perennial crops (the berries and grapes), rotates the annual crops, and lays wood chips, straw, or black plastic between the strawberry rows to keep down weeds.

17   His drip irrigation system—long plastic hoses buried in the ground with rubber tubes rising around each plant—trickles two to four gallons of water at the base of each grape and blueberry plant each night through the hot summer months. A separate sprinkler system waters the other crops from April to November. An electronic clock sends water through the acres of pipes daily and monitors the temperature. When the temperature drops below 34 degrees Fahrenheit, a fine film of water sprays the foliage. This sets up a cycle in which the water coating the plants turns to

Dwight Tilley and Booker T. Whatley (Photo by Manny Rubio)

ice that then melts again under the spray. Since heat is released when water changes from a liquid to a solid, the temperature of each plant is raised, staving off frost damage down to about 25 degrees.

18 Whatley also recommends a biological clock his grandfather used for frost control. "Pecan and other nut trees," Whatley wrote in one issue of his newsletter, "seldom get caught by late spring frost. When the leaves on a pecan tree reach the size of a squirrel's ear, then it's safe to plant tender crops like tomatoes and sweet potatoes."

19 Before any crop is planted, a test must determine the soil's pH—its acidity or alkalinity. The soil is then treated so that its pH suits each crop. "In Georgia, the state blueberry association recommends a boggy portion of the state, where the soil is acid, for growing blueberries because the pH is right to start with," Whatley says. "But they can grow blueberries all over that state if the pH is adjusted with sulfur and an ammonium sulfate fertilizer to make the soil more sour."

20 The McConnell Berry Farm, in the heart of Ohio's corn and soybean belt, practices on 195 acres much of what Whatley preaches. About 50 miles from Columbus, the farm originally grew strawberries, blueberries, and raspberries and added vegetables as a fail-safe against crop failure and to

please customers. Between May 1 and November 1 of last year, about 15,000 customer-pickers went through their gate. Owned by three families, the farm grosses over $300,000 a year and nets about $100,000.

21 "I wish I'd known about Whatley's idea when we were getting started," says George McConnell, one of the owners. "The money from a membership club would help a lot repaying our debt on the land."

22 While the McConnells have prospered as full-timers, many small farmers have hung on only by propping up their farms with a job in town. Others, called back-to-the-landers or Saturday-and-Sunday farmers, approach farming as a second and perhaps retirement career. These part-timers make up about 75 percent of all small farmers. But significantly, a new generation of young men and women have chosen full-time farming as a good life. Census figures show that the exodus from the farm ended in 1980. Then, for the first time since the 1930s, the number of small farms started to grow.

23 "They are all part of the small farm comeback," says Howard Kerr, until recently the agriculture department's small farm coordinator for the Northeast region. (He too is a part-timer, who grows peaches, blackberries, and strawberries on 15 acres.) Kerr believes Whatley's plan can help revitalize small farms.

24 But, as he points out, "Whatley's plan is for an expert, full-time farmer. Not all farmers can play by his rules. And not all farmers can run state-of-the-art Whatley farms. What about those farmers with about a seventh-grade education? Or those more than 40 miles from a city? Though Whatley dislikes the idea, some people need a middleman."

25 Fred Bennett, an Alabaman who has farmed for 38 years, agrees. "Farmers are way behind in marketing. Here in southeast Alabama we could accommodate hundreds of those types of farms. But I see two problems: being close enough to a city to get the customers and getting established. I'm 50 miles away from Montgomery and could never have borrowed the $75,000 it would have taken a cotton farmer like me to convert to a small farm."

26 But Fred Bennett's younger brothers are trying parts of Whatley's idea on the Bennetts' 2,200 acres. They're growing three or four acres of peas, some butter beans and squash, and about 12 acres of sweet potatoes along with 600 acres of wheat and potatoes. "Those are high yield-per-acre crops and they provide a more constant cash flow," says Fred Bennett, adding, "but we need a lot of help in selling what we know how to produce."

27 As Whatley so often complains, that help is unlikely to come from the government.

The agriculture department's current budget for small farm research is $1.1 million, down from $3.8 million the year before. It is scheduled to drop to $500,000 by 1990.

28   Since 1981 about 600 farmers have started up or converted to Whatley's program. Recently, he has enlisted "state coordinators" to visit farms and assemble detailed layouts of sites and acreage for each crop, complete with how and where to install the irrigation systems. The service costs $100, $80 of which goes to the coordinator. About 75 farmers requested coordinators in the first year.

29   John Sellens, a 37-year-old Sequim, Washington, farmer and Whatley's coordinator for the state, is establishing a Whatley farm on 28 acres. "I started with the premise that there was no money in small farming," he says, "but Whatley jarred my memory. He reminded me of a book I read a long time ago called *Five Acres and Independence* by M.G. Kains. Like Whatley, Kains said that the farmer needs something to sell every day. The good thing about Whatley's plan is that you can take from it what you want. It wouldn't work if that weren't true."

30   In the end, it is Whatley's instinct for practical solutions that makes farmers listen respectfully. Talking recently to beekeepers, Whatley offered his timetested prescription for pollinating blueberries by exploiting the honeybee's strong sense of smell.

31   "Around dusk," he said "pick a few blueberry flowers and boil them into a tea. Then, just at twilight, pour a cupful of the brew around the entrance of the hive. The next morning"—he laughed, his voice rising to a high delighted pitch and his hands soaring like the bees—"those bees will come roaring out of that hive like rockets targeted on those blueberries."

32   But then, mulling another of the swarm of details that bedevil all farmers, Whatley added: "But I still don't know the right *number* of bees for a blueberry bush. It's somewhere between three and seven. That's a problem they're still working on at the farm."

TRUE OR FALSE

Directions: *Decide if each of the following statements is true (T) or false (F) based on the selection.*

_____ **1.** According to Booker T. Whatley, in order to increase his or her chances for success, a small farmer must generate year-round cash flow by planting a variety of crops that do not compete with each other during planting and harvest.

_____ **2.** A small farmer following Whatley's plan doesn't need any full-time workers.

_____ **3.** The *Small Farm Technical Newsletter* tells small farmers when crops should be planted.

_____ **4.** Whatley relies on a combination of natural predators and synthetic pesticides known as "integrated pest management."

_____ **5.** Whatley recommends relying solely on a sprinkler-type irrigation system.

_____ **7.** Whatley's plan is suited to anyone who is interested in operating a small farm.

_____ **8.** It is possible to change the chemical composition of the soil in particular areas in order to grow crops that normally would not grow in these areas.

_____ **9.** In order to successfully sell their crops, small farmers must be more than 40 miles from a large city.

_____**10.** Whatley is very popular because of his common sense and practical ideas.

READING WORKSHEET

Directions: *After you have completed the true-or-false exercise, answer the following questions. You may refer to the selection if necessary.*

1. What is the purpose of paragraph 1?

_____

_____

2. According to Booker T. Whatley, what are the two necessities for the survival of a small farm?

a. _____

b. _____

3. In paragraph 3, we read, "Formally, his purpose was to." What does *formally* mean in this sentence?
   a. that Whatley has changed his mind
   b. that Whatley has a formal purpose
   c. that Whatley's initial purpose has changed

4. What is Whatley's "formula" for a successful small farm?

   _____

   _____

   _____

   _____

5. What do you think a "pick-your-own club" is? Why must members of this club pay an annual fee?

   _____

   _____

6. Explain what is meant by *a unique economic umbrella*.

   _____

   _____

   What three examples does Whatley give to illustrate this?

   a. _____

   b. _____

   c. _____

7. What are the criteria for choosing crops?

   a. _____

   b. _____

c. _____

8. There is a change in focus between paragraphs 8 and 9. What is the focus of paragraphs 1 through 8? What change do we see in

   paragraph 9? _____

   _____

9. What is the difference between Whatley's view and the government's view of the small farm?

   _____

   _____

   _____

10. In paragraph 11, Whatley mentions a prejudice that many people have had toward farmers. What is this prejudice?

    _____

    _____

11. What is the government's definition of a small farm? _____

    _____

    _____

12. What is Whatley's definition of a small farm? _____

    _____

13. What kind of man would be labeled _the guru of common sense?_

    _____

    What do you think a guru is? _____

14. What two approaches does Whatley use in his method of farming?

    a. _____

    b. _____

15. What is _pesticide_? _____

    What do you think _-cide_ means? _____

Write down other words ending with *-cide*.

a. _____

b. _____

c. _____

16. What is the focus of paragraphs 14 through 19?

_____

_____

Which is the topic sentence in paragraph 14 that states this focus?

_____

_____

17. What two solutions are given in paragraph 15?

a. _____

b. _____

18. In paragraph 16, the phrase *"scratching Mother Nature's back"* is in quotations. Why? _____

_____

19. The second sentence in paragraph 16 discusses perennial crops and annual crops. Berries and grapes are given as examples of perennials. Do these crops need to planted every year? _____

How do you know? _____

Give an example of an annual crop. _____

20. There is a definition in paragraph 17. Locate it and write it here.

_____

_____

21. Whatley refers to tomatoes and sweet potatoes as "tender crops." What does this mean? _____

22. There is a definition of a term in the first sentence of paragraph

19. Give the term and the definition.

_____

_____

23. In paragraph 20 we see the terms *gross* and *net*. These are economic terms that are considered opposites. What do these terms refer to?

_____

24. The last sentence in paragraph 24 is related to the main idea of paragraph 25. Considering this, what do you think a "middle-man" is?

_____

_____

25. What is the image that the author gives of Booker T. Whatley throughout the article?

_____

INFERENCE AND RESTATEMENT

Directions: Decide whether each of the following is a restatement (R), an inference (I), or a false statement (F) according to the selection. If the sentence is a restatement, locate the original in the selection and give the paragraph number where it is found.

_____ **1.** Whatley's plan for small farms, which has grown out of his experience as a farmer and from his scientific knowledge of modern farming technology, protects small farmers from failure.

_____ **2.** Small farmers cannot compete successfully with big farmers.

_____ **3.** Whatley advises reading nature's warnings in order to determine when the temperature will change.

_____ **4.** Government support is essential to the successful application of Whatley's plan.

_____ **5.** Not all farmers can use Whatley's plan.

_____ **6.** A variety of crops that together generate money throughout the year are necessary to small farms.

_____ **7.** Whatley has given hope to the small farmer.

_____ **8.** For many years, the government has had a negative view of farmers operating small farms.

_____ **9.** Basically, the same strategy for what and when to plant can be applied to small farms anywhere.

_____**10.** In this decade alone, hundreds of farmers have put Whatley's plan into action.

VOCABULARY FROM CONTEXT

Directions: *Using your knowledge and information from the text, answer the following questions. Refer to the selection while you work. Don't be afraid to guess.*

1. horticulturist (paragraph 3)
This term is used as an appositive (a short definition following a

noun) to describe Whatley. The suffix *-ist* means _____
(Hint: look at the last part of this sentence for more information.)

Horticulturist means _____.

2. supplant (paragraph 8)
The sentence containing this word is an example of parallel construction. In this case, two similar clauses (and verbs) are connected by *and*.

Supplant means _____

3. voracious (paragraph 15)
If a flock of guinea fowl will eat enough bugs to reduce the amount of pesticide needed by 80 percent, then

Voracious means _____.

4. trickles (paragraph 17)
As you read the sentence, notice the amount of water that each plant receives during the night. Check the beginning of the sentence to see how the water is delivered to the plants.

Trickle means _____.

5. staving off (paragraph 17)

Considering the context of paragraph 17, *staving off* means _____

_____ .

How do you know? _____

What clues did you find in the paragraph? _____

6. sour (paragraph 19)
This term generally is not associated with soil; it is usually used to describe taste (a lemon, for example).

Sour means _____ .

SKILLS CHECKUP: CLASSIFICATION OF IDEAS

Directions: *Mark each sentence with one of the following letters to show how (or if) it supports the thesis statement.*
Thesis (T)
Main Idea (M)
Supporting Information (S)
Example (E)
Irrelevant (I)

Paragraphs 1 through 8

_____ **1.** In order to be succesful, a farmer must plant a variety of crops.

_____ **2.** Crops should not compete with each other during planting and harvest.

_____ **3.** Since strawberries and peaches are harvested at the same time, it is not wise to plant both.

_____ **4.** Whatley encourages farmers to build on a paved road near a large city.

_____ **5.** A small farm has got to have high-value crops and year-round cash flow.

_____ **6.** Each acre of each crop planted has to bring in over $3,000 every year.

Paragraphs 14 through 19

_____ **1.** Many farms have tried out Whatley's ideas.

_____ **2.** Whatley's approach combines homespun solutions with the best of modern technology.

_____ **3.** Ladybugs and praying mantises are natural predators that are helpful to the farmer.

_____ **4.** It's time to plant various types of vegetables when the leaves of a nut tree grow to a certain size.

_____ **5.** Crops can be irrigated using a sprinkler system and a drip irrigation system developed by Whatley.

_____ **6.** Whatley advises reading nature's warnings in order to determine temperature changes.

_____ **7.** Whatley relies on a combination of natural predators and synthetic pesticides known as "integrated pest management."

SUMMARY

Directions: *Fill in the blanks so that the following summary is logical, grammatically correct, and accurate according to the selection.*

Booker T. Whatley, a horticulturist from the Tuskegee Institute, has developed a _____ for small farmers to help ensure against economic _____ if one or more of their crops _____. Traditionally, small _____ have limited production to one or two _____. Whatley believes that this is not the most effective _____ of land and almost certainly is a _____ for failure. Instead, he _____ that the small farmer devote his land and effort to about _____ crops with high values. His plan _____ that the crops all have different _____ and harvesting schedules so as to avoid _____ for labor. Some of the crops must _____ an income during the winter. The crops that Whatley chooses are not limited to plants. He recommends _____ for honey and pollination of other crops, quails and pheasants for meat and _____, even rabbits and _____.

The specific crops depend on the climate in which the farm is located. Whatley believes that under this plan, if one or two of the crops fail in any _____, the farmer's economic _____ will remain _____.

ESSAY QUESTIONS

Directions: In one to three paragraphs, answer the following questions using information from the selection to support your ideas.

1. Whatley's objectives for the small farm are that it have high-value crops and a year-round cash flow. Suggest ways in which these objectives might be reached.

2. The main market for the crops produced on a Whatley farm is a pick-your-own membership club. Explain how this club works and why it is important to the success of a small farm.

3. Whatley's method combines the newest technology with proven folk practices. Give two examples of such combinations from this selection and discuss their advantages over a completely modern and technological approach.

RELATED READING

AMBER WAVES OF STRAIN

U.S. farm bounty has grown into a burden

STEPHEN KOEPP

Across the farm belt last week, it was clear that another bumper crop is on the way. In Illinois, the corn is already seven feet high in spots and not close to topping out. Some corn is tasseling weeks ahead of schedule, and an early harvest is in prospect. Soybeans have also benefited from perfect weather; many plants are waist high and flowering ahead of time. Good, dry planting weather came early this year across Iowa and Nebraska, and even scattered flooding has not hurt the promise of a bountiful harvest. Elsewhere in the Midwest, it is much the same, a year so good that Dennis Vercler, news director of the Illinois Farm Bureau, calls it "absolutely phenomenal."

Yet the great bounty of U.S. agriculture continues to be a curse as well as a blessing. As the corn rises speedily, so does a forest of new silos that signals a crop-storage problem of epic proportions. All across the

(Matthew Naythons/Gamma-Liaison Agency)

corn belt, from Indiana to Nebraska and Missouri to Minnesota, a binge of bin and silo building is in full swing. Reason: by the end of summer, U.S. farmers and the Department of Agriculture will be buried under more excess wheat, corn, rice and other products than ever before in history. Last week the immensity of the surplus became clear in the marketplace, as commodities traders sent the price of corn futures plunging to $1.71 per bu., the lowest level in twelve years.

While farmers fret about how to store the huge harvest, much tougher questions will loom as unavoidably as tarpaulin-covered mountains of wheat. The unsentimental truth is that America's farm industry, once a source of pride and power, has become an economic burden. Because so many other countries have improved their agricultural output, maintaining America's vast farming capacity is now a costly exercise in excess. During fiscal 1986 the expense to taxpayers for supporting farm programs will reach, according to the Government's estimates, $24 billion—a 36 percent increase over last year. As exports shrivel and imports increase, the U.S. agricultural industry no longer even produces the hefty foreign exchange earnings that farmers once provided.

To put the situation in order, the Government is allowing thousands of farmers to fail but is spending billions to boost foreign sales and prop up incomes for those who survive. Yet the adjustment process is a bitter one that promises hardship not only for farm families but for the thousands of already troubled farm-oriented businesses, including machinery builders, petrochemical companies, seed producers and the mom-and-pop shops that keep small rural towns alive.

This year's corn crop will be the most dramatic example of U.S. agriculture's relentless surpluses. Because of the almost perversely ideal weather, with exactly the right amount of rain at the proper intervals, says Illinois' Vercler, "crop development is just about the best ever." Last year's corn crop was the largest in history, 8.9 billion bu., of which a record 5 billion bu. is left over in storage. The expected bumper harvest of 8 billion bu. this year, smaller in volume that 1985's because an increasing number of farmers have taken some acreage out of production to qualify for Government support programs, will send prices plummeting even further into the cellar.

Other vast surpluses abound. At the beginning of last month, the U.S. held 1.9 billion bu. of wheat, a record overstock, and 847 million bu. of soybeans, almost 40 percent more than at the same time last year. Kansas alone held 178.8 million bu. of grain sorghum, a livestock feed, almost 80 percent more than in June 1985. The U.S. is producing a huge excess of milk as well, a problem reduced only partly by the USDA's program this year to pay thousands of dairy farmers some $1.8 billion to send their herds to slaughter or export markets.

The Midwest's surplus is so stubbornly large that even this year's severe drought in the South will fail to boost depressed farm prices. The sad result: farmers in those states will face a double bind of low prices and small harvests, which could push many of them over the financial brink. Last week's heat wave, which reached 105° F in parts of the Carolinas, further scorched crops and killed more than 500,000 chickens. "This could put us completely out of business," laments Dairy Farmer Charlie Bouldin, of Chatham County, N.C., who expects less than 30 percent of his hay and corn crops to survive.

But for most farmers, the problem is a lack of customers. Foreign sales of U.S. farm products have faltered because dozens of countries from Brazil to China have become more self-sufficent, while heavily indebted Third World nations lack the money to buy significant imports. This year total U.S. farm exports are expected to dip to $27.5 billion, down 12 percent from fiscal 1985 and 37 percent from 1981. At the same time, U.S. imports of such products as fish, fruit and vegetables have increased. Earlier this month the USDA announced that during May the U.S. became a net importer of farm products for the first time since 1959, except for occasions when dockworkers were on strike. May's farm deficit was $348.7 million. Although the USDA predicts a $7.5 billion agricultural-trade surplus for the year as a whole, the historic one-month deficit outraged farm-state legislators. Said Senate Majority Leader Robert Dole of Kansas: "Something is radically wrong when the greatest food producer in the world is buying more agricultural commodities than it is selling. This trend simply cannot continue."

The best hope for boosting exports at the moment is the Food Security Act of 1985, the farm legislation passed by Congress last December. The act allows the Government to lower agricultural price supports and thereby make U.S. products cheaper in foreign markets. The new farm policy, however, is proving very costly. To compensate farmers for lowered price supports, the law provides dramatic increases in so-called deficiency payments, which are given directly to farmers to ensure that their net incomes remain stable. Under the new plan, farmers will generally derive a larger portion of their income, typically more than a third, from the Government. As a result, budget-cutting pressure could force the program to be scaled back next year in Congress. Moreover, the dramatic increase in U.S. farm subsidies fans protectionist sentiment in other countries.

The subsidies, however, are backed by many farm-state voters with an understandably desperate zeal. More than 50,000 of the country's 2.3 million farmers hung up their tractor keys for good during 1985, and 50,000 more will probably be forced to quit this year. Says Enid Schlipf, who grows corn in Gridley Township, Ill.: "If a farmer's got a lot of debt, he's in deep trouble, no matter how good an operator he is." Foreclosures and bankruptcy have devastated the morale of many lifetime farmers and spurred at least a score of heartland suicides. Last week a 54-year-old farmwife in Chattanooga, Okla., despondent over her family's debts on their 1,280-acre wheat-and-cotton operation, killed herself by climbing atop a barrel of burning trash.

The financial strain has been aggravated by a get-tough lending policy at the Farmers Home Administration, the federal agency that makes and guarantees agricultural loans, and the Farm Credit System, a network of more than 600 banks and credit associations. Both organizations have adopted a more stringent policy, cutting off the most overextended farmers. The FCS suffered a loss of $2.7 billion last year, and holds some $12 billion in problem loans on its books. Says FHA Administrator Vance Clark: "We're going to lose a lot of farmers this year, and we've got to accept that."

Besides farm lenders, thousands of other businesses have suffered ripple effects. Tractor sales, for example, totaled only 58,500 in 1985, compared with 139,000 during the last good year, 1979. The slump has prompted several famous manufacturers to leave the business. Milwaukee's Allis-Chalmers, New York's Sperry and Chicago's International Harvester (renamed Navistar International) have sold their farm-machinery operations to competitors, a consolidation trend that has caused tens of thousands of employee layoffs. Of some 20 farm-equipment dealers who prospered in McLean County, Ill., five years ago, only three remain.

Some of the more optimistic farmers think they see a few rays of dawn on the horizon. The continuing decline of interest rates, for example, makes it easier for them to meet payments of their land and equipment. Falling prices for fertilizers, seed and other supplies have helped too, by reducing farm expenses. Finally, the falling value of the U.S. dollar should make farm exports more affordable for foreigners. But it will take the U.S. a long time to sell off the surpluses it has produced. Those rays of dawn are still barely visible through the lush, tall cornstalks.

Reported by Gisela Bolte/Washington and Lee Griggs/Des Moines

DISCUSSION

1. Why does a large harvest equal economic failure for many U.S. farmers?

2. Why do you think the United States imports fruits and vegetables from other countries when many of its own farmers are having financial difficulties?

3. Do you believe that a government should support an industry that produces more than it can sell, as the American government does with farm commodities? What underlying economic reasons do you see for this action?

4. Some people believe that large farms that produce only two or three major crops should be owned by big business rather than by individual farm families. Do you agree with this point of view?

5. This selection contains a number of synonyms for *rise* and *fall*. Look for these words with your teacher.

9

Consumer
Needs
and
Motivation

RELATED READING

PRICEY ICE CREAM IS SCOOPING THE MARKET

Myron Jennings, manager of BiLo supermarket No. 119 in Spartanburg, S.C., knows why Frusen Glädjé ice cream—priced at $2 a pint—is the hottest item in his freezer chest: "It's the quality and the name. People don't care what it costs."

Such dedication by customers is propelling growth in superpremium ice creams by about 20 percent annually. It's enough to make mouths water in the sluggish food business. That's why giant packaged-goods marketers such as Dart & Kraft Inc. and Pillsbury Co., which have scooped up the largest positions in the super-premium ice cream market, are pulling out all stops to expand sales. They are launching aggressive advertising campaigns and rolling out a host of new products to bring mass marketing to what traditionally has been a mom-and-pop industry. Smaller rivals are fighting back with new products and promotional efforts of their own.

Tasting Success

Pillsbury, which owns market leader Häagen-Dazs, is now cranking out new sorbet-and-cream flavors. That followed the February introduction of Häagen-Dazs ice cream bars, which are coated with Belgian chocolate. National advertising for the brand began in December. Häagen-Dazs sales, which reached about $175 million for the year ending in May, have more than doubled since Pillsbury acquired the company for $76 million in 1983.

Dart & Kraft brought Frusen Glädjé just a year ago. But it has already tripled the brand's market share. The gains came in part because of a fat advertising budget that uses "enjoy the guilt" as its theme. In one commercial, a woman is eating Frusen Glädjé as her husband comes home. She confesses she has finished the entire container. She looks guilty for a moment, then adds: "And I'd do it again." Thomas Herskovits, president of Kraft's dairy division, says the ads "capture the essence of the indulgent product it is."

Indulgence sells a lot of ice cream these days. While the business has remained flat overall, sales of super-premiums—which contain twice the butterfat of regular ice cream, less air, and generally only natural ingredients—have doubled since 1980. This is now a $1.9 billion market, according to Find/SVP, a New York-based research firm. It projects that superpremium sales will grow at double-digit rates through 1990.

Consumers are attracted by the ice creams' taste, quality, and classy image. The products have European-sounding names, although they are as American as apple pie. Häagen-Dazs, which is a made-up name, was created and initially manufactured in the Bronx. Frusen Glädjé, Swedish for frozen dessert, has always been produced domestically. That doesn't seem to bother consumers. They pay an average $2 per pint for superpremiums and about that for a double-dipped cone at the local "gourmet" ice cream parlor. In contrast, a premium ice cream such as Breyer's or Dreyer's sells for about $4 a half gallon.

To ensure that customers can always get their fill of flavors such as Vanilla Swiss Almond and Elberta Peach, Pillsbury and Kraft have built new plants and added the pricey ice creams to their supermarket routes. Herskovits estimates 70 percent of the nation's supermarkets now carry superpremiums, up from just 45 percent a year ago. Seeing the success of Pillsbury and Kraft, other packaged-good companies—notably General Mills Inc. and Campbell Soup Co.—are studying the market. The industry is "very open," says Häagen-Dazs president Mark Stevens. "Anybody can launch a new brand or open a store."

Getting started in the business is one thing, but as competition grows more intense, staying in it is something else. "The smaller companies just don't have the supermarket clout and the wherewithal to develop and introduce new products on a large scale like Pillsbury and Kraft," says ice cream expert Arun Kilara, a Pennsylvania State University food-science professor. "Since everyone is looking to get on the superpremium bandwagon, the smaller companies will find it harder and harder to survive."

Amateur Experts

Those who do will have to differentiate their products and obtain the necessary capital to compete. One way to do that is by going public, the route taken by Ben & Jerry's Homemade Inc. Ben Cohen and Jerry Greenfield, then both 28, founded the company in 1978. There was no grand design. At the time, Greenfield was a lab technician and Cohen a potter. "We both wanted to quit our jobs, and we both liked to eat," Cohen recalls, adding that they had experience. "Jerry scooped ice cream in the food line at high school, and I drove one of those ice-cream trucks with a bell."

While this would hardly set venture capitalists' hearts aflutter, the Vermont-based company managed to raise a total of $7.25 million in public offerings in 1984 and 1985. The stock now trades at 24—60 times earnings and up 85 percent from the initial offering price. The new money allowed the company to expand on the East Coast. Ben & Jerry's made $550,000 last year on sales of $9.7 million. Success may stem in part from its anticorporate image: Ben & Jerry's donates 15 percent of earnings to charity, proclaims that its lowest-paid employee earns at least 20 percent of the best-paid worker's salary, and shows free films outdoors in many cities where its ice cream is sold.

Cohen argues that large competitors will help his company. "Somebody in Enosburg Falls, Vermont, isn't going to want an ice cream with some foreign-sounding name," he says.

Officials at DoveBar International Inc., a Chicago-based superpremium company, hope their headstart in making ice cream bars —and an innovative new product—will stave off rivals. The privately held company, formed in 1983, sold 184,000 DoveBars—6 oz. of choco-late-coated ice cream on a stick—in 1984 and 7.5 million last year. DoveBar had sales of $5.5 million in 1985. President Louis G. Yaseen won't disclose earnings but says profits are "handsome."

This year, DoveBar projects sales of 35 million units. That includes both DoveBars and its new product, Dove-Delight—a 3.25-oz. ice-cream sundae. The company also just launched its first advertising campaign. DoveBar will spend $3.5 million to recall its history humorously. In one ad, Michael L. Stefanos, son of founder Leo Stefanos and now a company executive, explains: "The moment my dad said, 'Son, I've invented the DoveBar,' I knew I wasn't going to grow up to be a veterinarian."

Even strong competitors such as DoveBar and Ben & Jerry's, however, must respond to the big boys. Both companies want to remain independent, but they may be forced to merge the larger companies that have deeper pockets and better distribution networks. Small regionals such as Double Rainbow Gourmet Ice Cream Inc. in San Francisco and Baltimore-based Mellin Foods Co., which makes the Apres brand, may face a similar fate. Many find it hard to break into the supermarket freezer because they lack the needed distribution and ad budgets. And ironically, cutting prices to compete might not help. Part of a superpremium's appeal to consumers is its high price. With Pillsbury and Kraft expecting to grow faster than the market as a whole, the smaller companies may see their market share melt away.

By Paul B. Brown in New York, with Kenneth Dreyfack in Chicago, Alex Beam in Boston, Mary J. Pitzer in Minneapolis, Kimberly Carpenter in Philadelphia, and Joan O'C. Hamilton in San Francisco

—Reprinted from June 30, 1986 issue of *Business Week* by special permission, © 1986 by McGraw-Hill, Inc.

DISCUSSION

Directions: *Read the following questions. Be prepared to discuss them.*

1. Why do you think people are willing to spend so much money on ice cream?

2. What does the following statement mean to you: "Indulgence sells a lot of ice cream"?

3. Why are consumers so attracted to expensive ice cream?

4. How do you think a "classy image" is portrayed in advertising?

5. How do you think the public is being fooled by ice cream advertisements?

6. What kind of image do Ben and Jerry wish to portray? Why?

Prereading

DISCUSSION

Directions: Read the following questions. Be prepared to discuss them.

1. What do you think is meant by *consumer needs and motivation?*

2. What fields of study would be interested in why people buy certain things?

3. Discuss your motivation for these behaviors: attending a university, getting married, buying a new car.

4. What are some of your personal goals for today? this week? this year?

5. Think of something that you have bought recently. Why did you buy it? Did you buy a particular brand? What influenced your decision to buy that brand?

PREVIEW

Directions: Read the title and any subheadings of the selection. Also look at the illustrations and read any captions. Then, without reading the selection, answer the following questions.

1. What paragraphs make up the introduction to the unit?

2. What is the definition of *motivation?*

3. What are the two types of motives?

4. Look at Figure 9–1. What kind of relationship is being portrayed?
   a. comparison and contrast
   b. cause and effect
   c. classification

5. This type of organization of events in Figure 9-1 is called a *cycle.*
   Why do you think it is called this?
   What begins or sets off this chain?
   What two things affect behavior?

READING

CONSUMER NEEDS AND MOTIVATION

1   We have all grown up "knowing" that people are different. They seek different pleasures, spend their money in different ways. A couple may spend their vacation traveling in Europe; their friends are content with two weeks in a cottage by the sea. A doting father may buy his son a set of encyclopedias; another may buy his son a set of electric trains. A woman may save her household money to carpet her bedrooms; her neighbor may save hers to buy a second car. Different modes of consumer behavior—different ways of spending money—do not surprise us. We have been brought up to believe that the differences in people are what makes life interesting.

2   However, this apparent diversity in human behavior often causes us to overlook the fact that people are really very much alike. There are underlying similarities—*constants* that tend to operate across many types of people—which serve to explain and to clarify their consumption behavior. Psychologists and consumer behaviorists agree that basically most people experience the same kinds of needs and motives; they simply express these motives in different ways. For this reason, an understanding of human motives is very important to marketers: It enables them to understand, and even anticipate, human behavior in the marketplace.

3   This chapter will discuss the basic needs that operate in most people to motivate behavior. It explores the influence that such needs have on consumption behavior . . . .

What Is Motivation

Motivation

4   Several basic concepts are integral to an understanding of human motivation. Before we discuss these, it is necessary to agree on some basic definitions. *Motivation* can be described as *the driving force within individuals that impels them to action*. This driving force is produced by a state of tension, which exists as the result of an unfilled need. Individuals strive—both consciously and subconsciously—to reduce this tension through behavior that they anticipate will fulfill their needs and thus relieve them of the stress they feel. The specific goals they select and the patterns of action they undertake to achieve their goals are the results of individual thinking and learning. Figure 9–1 presents a model of the motivational process. It portrays motivation as a state of need-induced tension, which exerts a "push" on the

"Understanding human needs is half the job of meeting them."
—Adlai Stevenson: Speech, Columbus, Ohio (October 3, 1952)

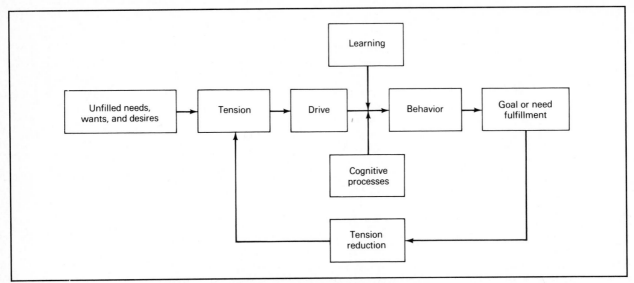

Figure 9–1. A Model of the Motivation Process

individual to engage in behavior that he or she expects will gratify needs and thus reduce tension. Whether gratification is actually achieved depends on the course of action pursued. (If a high-school girl pins her hopes of being asked to the senior prom on her switch to a highly advertised "sexy" toothpaste, she may be disappointed. If her brother pins his hopes of making the tennis team on his purchase of a tennis racquet endorsed by Vitas Gerulaitis, he too may be disappointed.)

5   The specific courses of action undertaken by consumers and the specific goals chosen are selected on the basis of their thinking processes (i.e., cognition) and previous learning. Thus marketers who understand motivational theory attempt to influence the consumer's thinking or cognitive processes.

Needs

6   Every individual has needs; some are innate, others are acquired. Innate needs are physiological (i.e.,

biogenic); they include the needs for food, for water, for air, for clothing, for shelter, and for sex. Because all of these factors are needed to sustain biological life, the biogenic needs are considered *primary* needs or motives.

7   Acquired needs are needs that we learn in response to our culture or environment. These may include needs for esteem, for prestige, for affection, for power, and for learning. Because acquired needs are generally psychological (i.e., psychogenic), they are considered *secondary* needs or motives. They result from the individual's subjective psychological state and from his or her relationships with others. For example, all individuals need shelter from the elements; thus, finding a place to live fulfills an important primary need for a newly transferred executive. However, the kind of house she buys may be the result of secondary needs. She may seek a house where she can entertain large groups of people (and fulfill her social needs); furthermore, she may want to buy a house in an exclusive community in order

to impress her friends and family (and fulfill her ego needs). The house that an individual ultimately purchases thus may serve to fulfill both primary and secondary needs.

Goals

8   Goals are the sought-after results of motivated behavior. As Figure 9–1 indicates, all behavior is goal-oriented. Our discussion of motivation in this chapter is in part concerned with consumers' *generic* goals; that is, the general classes or categories of goals they select to fulfill their needs. Marketers are even more concerned with consumers' *product-specific* goals; that is, the specifically branded or labeled products they select to fulfill their needs. For example, the Thomas J. Lipton Company wants consumers to view iced tea as a good way to quench summer thirst (i.e., as a generic goal). However, it is even more interested in having consumers view *Lipton's* iced tea as the *best* way to quench summer thirst (i.e., as a product-specific goal). As trade association advertising indicates, marketers recognize the importance of promoting both types of goals. The American Dairy Association advertises that "milk is a natural," while Borden's, a member of the Association, advertises its own brand of milk.

Positive and Negative Motivation

9   Motivation can be either positive or negative in direction. We may feel a driving force *toward* some object or condition, or a driving force *away* from some object or condition. For example, a person may be impelled toward a restaurant to fulfill a hunger need and away from airplane transportation to fulfill a safety need. Some psychologists refer to positive drives as needs, wants or desires, and negative drives as fears or aversions. However, though negative and positive motivational forces seem to differ dramatically in terms of physical (and sometimes emotional) activity, they are basically similiar in that they both serve to initiate and sustain human behavior. For this reason, researchers often refer to both kinds of drives or motives as needs, wants, and desires.

10   Goals, too, can be either positive or negative. A positive goal is one toward which behavior is directed, and thus it is often referred to as an *approach* object. A negative goal is one from which behavior is directed away, and thus it is sometimes referred to as an *avoidance* object. Since both approach and avoidance goals can be considered objectives of motivated behavior, most researchers refer to both types simply as *goals*. Consider this example. A middle-aged woman may wish to remain as attractive as possible to male acquaintances. Her positive goal is to appear desirable, and therefore she may use a perfume advertised to make her "irresistible." A negative goal may be to prevent her skin from aging, and therefore she may buy and use face creams advertised to prevent wrinkles. In the former case, she uses perfume to help her achieve her positive goal—sexual attractiveness; in the latter case, she uses face creams to help avoid a negative goal—wrinkled skin.

The Selection of Goals

11 For any given need, there are many different and appropriate goals. The goals selected by individuals depend on their personal experiences, physical capacity, prevailing cultural

norms and values, and the goal's accessibility in the physical and social environment. For example, an individual may have a strong hunger need. If he is a young American athlete, he may envision a rare sirloin steak as his goal-object; however, if he is also an orthodox Jew, he may require that the steak be kosher to conform to Jewish dietary laws. If the individual is old or infirm, he may not have the physical capacity to chew or digest a steak; therefore, he may select hamburger instead. If he has never tasted steak—if it is out of his realm of personal experience—he will probably not even think of steak as a goal-object but instead will select a food that has satified his hunger before (perhaps fish or chicken).

12   Finally, the goal-object has to be both physically and socially accessible. If the individual were shipwrecked on an island with no food provisions or living animals, he could not realistically select steak as his goal-object, though he might fantasize about it. If he were in India where cows are considered sacred deities, he could not realistically hope to consume steak because to do so might be considered sacrilegious. Therefore he would have to select a substitute goal more appropriate to the social environment.

13   The individual's own conception of himself or herself also serves to influence the specific goals selected. The products that a person owns, would like to own, or would not like to own are often perceived in terms of how closely they reflect (are congruent with) the person's self-image. A product that is perceived as fitting an individual's self-image has a greater probability of being selected than one that is not. Thus a man who perceives himself as young and "swinging" may drive a Corvette; a

woman who perceives herself as rich and conservative may drive a Mercedes. The types of houses people live in, the cars they drive, the clothes they wear, the very foods they eat—these specific goal-objects are often chosen because symbolically they reflect the individual's own self-image while they satisfy specific needs. . . .

Rational versus Emotional Motives

14   Some consumer researchers distinguish between so-called rational motives and emotional (or nonrational) motives. They use the term *rationality* in the traditional economic sense that assumes that consumer behave rationally when they carefully consider all alternatives and choose those that give them the greatest utility (i.e., satisfaction). In a marketing context, the term *rationality* implies that the consumer selects goals based on totally objective criteria, such as size, weight, price, or miles per gallon. *Emotional* motives imply the selection of goals according to personal or subjective criteria (the desire for individuality, pride, fear, affection, status).

15   The assumption underlying this distinction is that subjective or emotional criteria do not maximize utility or satisfaction. However, it is reasonable to assume that consumers always attempt to select alternatives that, *in their view,* serve to maximize satisfaction. Obviously, the assessment of satisfaction is a very personal process, based upon the individual's own need structure as well as on past behavioral, social, and learning experiences. What may appear as irrational to an outside observer may be perfectly rational within the context of the consumer's own psychological field. For example, a product pur-

chased to enhance one's self-image (such as a fragrance) is a perfectly rational form of consumer behavior. If behavior did not appear rational to the person who undertakes it at the time that it is undertaken, obviously he or she would not do it. Therefore the distinction between rational and emotional motives does not appear to be warranted.

16   Indeed, some researchers go so far as to suggest that emphasis on "needs" obscures the rational, or conscious, nature of most consumer motivation. They claim that consumers act consciously to maximize their gains and minimize their losses; that they act not from subconscious drives but from rational preferences, or what they perceive to be in their own best interests.

17   Marketers who agree with this view are reluctant to spend either time or money to uncover subconscious buyer motives. Instead, they try to identify problems that consumers ex-

perience with products then on the market. For example, instead of trying to identify any special needs that consumers may have for dog food, the marketer wil try to discover any problems that consumers are experiencing with existing brands of dog food. If the marketer discovers that many dog foods leave an unpleasant order in the refrigerator, he or she can develop a new product that solves this consumer problem and then run advertisements that announce to dog owners that the new product does not impart unpleasant odors. Thus, rather than address consumers' expressed needs, such marketers attempt to discover and solve consumers' problems and thereby achieve market success.

—Schiffman/Kanuk, *Consumer Behavior*, 2/E, © 1983, pp. 48–52. Reprinted by permission of Prentice-Hall, Inc., Englewood Cliffs, New Jersey.

Postreading

TRUE OR FALSE

Directions: Decide if each of the following statements is true (T) or false (F) based on the selection.

_____ 1. Because most people have similar needs and motives, marketers are able to predict how consumers will behave in the marketplace.

_____ 2. A primary need, like the need for water, is physiological, while a secondary need, like the need for power, is biogenic.

_____ 3. One goal may fulfill both a primary and secondary need.

_____ 4. A person who will only wear Levi's jeans probably is fulfilling a secondary need with a product-specific goal.

_____ 5. All of us have drives that are positive or negative in direction.

_____ 6. Positive motives usually result in the feeling of contentment, while negative motives most often result in feelings of disappointment.

_____ 7. A negative goal is a "could be" result that a person does not want.

_____ 8. Even though many people experience the same need, they choose different goals depending on only one thing: their personal experiences.

_____ 9. A person who spends much more money than his income provides for is behaving rationally.

_____10. What is rational to one person may be perceived as irrational by another.

READING WORKSHEET

Directions: After you have completed the true-or-false exercise, answer the following questions. You may refer to the selection if necessary.

1. Look at paragraphs 1 through 3. These paragraphs serve to intro-

duce the chapter. Which paragraph discusses the content of this chapter? _____

2. Reread paragraph 1. Which sentence is the topic sentence?

_____

_____

3. Reread the first sentence in paragraph 2. What kind of information is signaled by *however*? What does *this apparent diversity* refer to in the first sentence of paragraph 2? _____

4. Locate the dashes (—) in paragraph 2. What is their purpose?
   a. to define
   b. to give an example of
   c. to restate information

5. Read the last sentence in paragraph 2. What does *for this reason* refer to? _____
   This phrase is used as a transition between a cause and effect. What is the cause? _____
   What is the effect? _____

6. Read the quotation by Adlai Stevenson. Explain it. _____

_____

7. Read paragraph 4 and look at Figure 9–1.
   What is another term for *driving force*? _____
   What produces this driving force? _____
   According to the example given in this paragraph, will gratification of needs necessarily be achieved? _____
   What does gratification depend on? _____
   In the example of the high school girl and her brother, what are the unfilled needs?

   a. _____

   b. _____

What are the modes of behavior?

a. _____

b. _____

8. What do marketers want to influence? Why? _____

_____

9. What are primary needs? _____
Give some examples. _____

_____

10. What are secondary needs? _____
Give some examples. _____

11. Label the following as a primary need, a secondary need, or both.

water _____

beer _____

books _____

love _____

dress _____

Describe why a dress might fulfill both a primary and secondary
need. _____

_____

12. What is the definition of *goal* as given in the text? _____

_____

What is a synonym of *goal* used in this definition? _____
There is a cause/effect relationship expressed within this definition.

What is the cause? _____

What is the effect? _____

13. What are the two kinds of goals?

a. _____

b. _____

Label the following as either (a) or (b).

blue jeans _____

Levi blue jeans _____

What about "chewing gum"? _____

Give an example of a product-specific goal in relation to chewing

gum. _____

14. The author states that there are two types of motivation:

_____ and _____. How do these motivational forces differ?

a. _____

b. _____

Label the following as positive (P) or negative (N) drives.

a. __N__ walking on the sidewalk in order to stay away from moving vehicles

b. _____ taking the stairs instead of using a very old elevator

c. _____ walking in to a shoe store in order to buy a new pair of snow boots

d. _____ buying a new book about economics

e. _____ buying a weight-lifting set in order to become strong

What do the above examples fulfill?

a. the need for safety

b. _____

c. _____

d. _____

e. _____

15. What is an approach object? _____

What is an avoidance object? _____

16. Label each of the following as an approach or avoidance object. Explain your answer.

using face creams _____

using perfume _____

17. What does *former* mean in paragraph 10? _____

What does *latter* mean? _____

18. What factors affect an individual's choice of goals? _____

_____

19. What does *he* refer to in the last sentence of paragraph 11?

_____

20. The first word of paragraph 12 is _____. What is the purpose

of this word? _____

21. What does *fantasize* mean in paragraph 12?
   a. forget
   b. wish
   c. talk
   c. dream

22. Why is the word *also* used in the first sentence of paragraph 13?

_____

What is the author adding information to? _____

23. Paragraph 14 serves
   a. to introduce the terminology that will be used in further
      paragraphs.
   b. as a transition paragraph between paragraphs 13 and 15.
   c. to summarize the preceding paragraphs.

24. Locate the first sentence in paragraph 15. What does *this distinction*

refer to? _____

25. Why is *in their view* (paragraph 15) printed in italics? _____

_____

INFERENCE AND RESTATEMENT

*Directions: Decide whether each of the following is a restatement (R), an infer-
ence (I), or a false statement (F) according to the selection. If the sentence is a
restatement, locate the original in the selection and give the paragraph number
where it is found.*

_____ **1.** The action a person takes will determine if his or her need will be met.

_____ **2.** A person who buys a very expensive fur coat probably is trying to fulfill some psychogenic need.

_____ **3.** A person who avoids deep water because he can't swim is being motivated by a negative drive.

_____ **4.** An individual's personal history, age, condition of health, and social training as well as the availability of a particular goal-object play a large role in that individual's choice of goals.

_____ **5.** People often make purchases based on what they see as non-rational motives.

_____ **6.** Sellers often try to increase their sales by offering "new and improved" products to consumers.

_____ **7.** The act of buying popcorn at the movies may be motivated by either a biogenic or a psychological need.

_____ **8.** It is unnecessary for the designer of a new product to examine whether the needs of potential consumers are rational or non-rational.

_____ **9.** Consumer behavior is not always goal oriented.

_____**10.** All of us have some needs that we are born with and others that we learn.

VOCABULARY FROM CONTEXT

Directions: _Using your own knowledge and information from the text, answer the following questions. Refer to the selection while you work. Don't be afraid to guess._

1. diversity (paragraph 2)
   Examples explaining the meaning of this word are given in paragraph 1.

   Diversity means _____.

2. integral (paragraph 4)
   A synonym for this word is given in the second sentence in this paragraph.

   Integral means _____.

3. impels (paragraph 4)

The definition in which this word appears gives you a clue to its meaning.

Impels means _____.

4. cognition (paragraph 5)

An explanation or other term is given for this word in the same sentence.

Cognition means _____.

5. innate (paragraph 6)

An antonym (word with an opposite meaning) for this word is given in the same sentence.

Innate means _____.

6. aversion (paragraph 9)

An antonym for this word is given in the same sentence.

aversion means _____.

SKILLS CHECKUP: CLASSIFICATION OF IDEAS

Directions: *Mark each sentence with one of the following letters to show how (or if) it supports the thesis statement.*
Thesis (T)
Main Idea (M)
Supporting Information (S)
Example (E)
Irrelevant (I)

_____ **1.** Biogenic needs (air, light, water, food, shelter, and sex) are common to all people.

_____ **2.** Psychogenic needs (power, affection, acceptance, etc.) vary among individuals.

_____ **3.** Differences in age, sex, nationality, ethnic background, and personal experience determine psychogenic needs.

_____ **4.** Consumer behavior is motivated by unfulfilled biogenic and psychogenic needs.

_____ **5.** Advertisers are more concerned with our psychogenic needs.

_____ **6.** Motivation can be either negative or positive.

_____ **7.** Everyone must have food to eat; so, in order to get the consumer to eat in a certain expensive restaurant, satisfaction of some psychogenic need, such as prestige, must be offered.

_____ **8.** Often a consumer's need is based on his or her self-image.

_____ **9.** Manufacturers often study products that already are on the market to determine their weaknesses and then offer a similar product that lacks those weaknesses.

_____**10.** A man who considers himself a good tennis player, will choose a tennis racquet that reflects this image.

_____**11.** People buy products that reinforce their perceptions of themselves.

_____**12.** Marketers try to influence the thinking patterns of buyers.

SUMMARY

Directions: _Write a summary of the selection. Include as many of the following words and phrases (or their related forms) as you wish. Begin with this sentence: All human behaviors are motivated by tensions that result from unfulfilled needs._

consumer	acquired	psychogenic
advertiser	prestige	spend
innate	power	perception

ESSAY QUESTIONS

Directions: _In one to three paragraphs, answer the following questions using information from the selection to support your ideas._

1. Consumer behavior is based upon the motivation to meet unfulfilled needs. Discuss whether meeting the consumer's biogenic needs should be more important to the marketer and why.

2. To what consumer need do you think an advertiser is appealing when he or she shows rich and sophisticated people in a car commercial?

3. Discuss how our social norms and values influence our attempts to meet our biogenic needs. Support your answers with examples.

10 Clocks that Make Us Run

RELATED READING

THE RAVAGES OF TIME

Business travel and shifts in work schedules take their toll on your body. But diet and rest can help.

RICHARD J. CHAPEL

You don't have to be a globe-hopping executive to experience jet lag. Crossing more than two time zones is often enough to disrupt your body's normal day–night rhythm. Similarly, changing work shifts generally raises havoc with many biological cycles that are regulated by an internal "clock."

Researchers have shown that most of our clocks run on a 25-hour cycle instead of 24. The extra hour gives our bodies a "cushion" for adjusting to minor schedule changes. External prompts such as light, dark and meal-times regulate our internal timers. As long as these cues are not much out of phase with the internal clock, resetting is easy, and body rhythms remain regular. Shift the external cues by as much as an hour, and the internal timing experiences a "lag"—it can't catch up fast enough.

So, the problem with multiple time zone changes and the resulting jet lag is that, during the adjustment period, not only are you out of phase with people and events, but some of your own internal functions may

be out of phase with each other. The same principle is at work when you change shifts on the job.

For the business executive who expects to perform at peak efficiency upon arrival at a destination, jet lag is more than a travel side effect. Indeed, it can be considered a major liability. Likewise, workers struggling to adjust to a new work shift are not in a condition to perform at peak efficiency. It is no wonder that business is showing a strong interest in research into methods of adjusting to time shifts.

Lt. Col. Curtis Graeber is leading a team of researchers investigating multiple time shift displacement at the National Aeronautics and Space Administration's Ames Research Center in California. His research has identified a body temperature rhythm that strongly influences ability to sleep. "We now know that a rising body temperature will cause you to awaken, no matter how tired you are," he says. "The rise and fall of body temperatures is one of the master internal clocks." Graeber says that the cycle may take days to adjust itself, so the key to dealing with a time shift is to fight it effectively.

Planning for an impending time zone displacement is something business travelers

do not do very well. Graeber says. "We've found that people just don't handle the day before departure properly. They start out behind the eight ball by cramming in last-minute work. You should minimize the last-minute rush. Don't get on the plane exhausted and expecting to sleep. Your internal body temperature cycle may not allow it."

Graeber says that a new prescription drug may offer a means of getting needed sleep—in spite of an out-of-phase internal clock: "The generic name for this drug is triazolan. It helps you achieve a sound sleep for 4 to 5 hours and rapidly clears out your system. For short trips where adjustment can't take place naturally, triazolan is effective."

Charles F. Ehret, a biologist with the Argonne National Laboratory in Illinois, is the author of a book entitled *Overcoming Jet Lag*. The book has received a lot of publicity because of a diet that Ehret says is effective against jet lag.

Adjusting to the disruptions of jet lag or shift work involves more than dietary changes, Ehret says. "The diet is just a focal point, but with it, travelers can adjust to as many as five zones within a day after landing."

The diet, which must be

started three days before a trip, involves a pattern of "feast" and "fast" days. It sounds complicated, but Ehret has summarized the diet on a pocket card he sends out on request. Send a stamped, self-addressed envelope to Anti-Jet-Lag Diet. Argonne National Laboratory, 9700 S. Cass Avenue, Argonne, Ill. 60439.

For combating jet lag, sleep is important, but research indicates other adaptive measures can also help you deal with time zone changes:

1. Start your trip rested.
2. En route, avoid caffeine and alcohol. Drink juice or water.
3. Avoid candy or other high sugar foods. Have fruit or nuts instead.
4. At your destination, assume the pattern of the new time zone. Get outside and stay active. Sleep according to your new "clock."
5. Plan for jet lag. Knowing that your performance may be reduced the first day, you should schedule lightly.

Time shifts decrease alertness and ability to concentrate. Warding off jet lag may require special "travel training" combining dietary adjustments and physical fitness. Successful business travel may indeed be a matter of the survival of the fittest.

—Reprinted by permission from *Nation's Business*, November 1985. Copyright 1985, U.S. Chamber of Commerce.

Richard J. Chapel is a free-lance writer from Worcester, Mass.

DISCUSSION

Directions: Read the following questions. Be prepared to discuss them.

1. According to the article, what two things can cause problems with your biological cycles?
   a.
   b.

2. What environmental changes affect your internal clocks?

3. How does a change in these external prompts affect a person?

4. What does the author mean by *lag*?

5. Why are businesses interested in finding out more about time shifts?

6. What biological cycle may be the most important in controlling our sleep patterns?

7. Why do you think a person should avoid sugar, caffeine, and alcohol when traveling to another time zone?

8. Have you ever experienced jet lag? Can you describe how you were affected physically and psychologically?

Prereading

DISCUSSION

Directions: Read the following questions. Be prepared to discuss them.

1. If you wanted to lose weight, how would you change your eating habits? Do you think that the time of day when you eat affects weight gain or loss? If so, when would be the best time to eat your biggest meal? Why?

2. Do drugs affect you differently when taken at different times of day? For example, will drinking a glass of wine have a different effect in the morning as compared to the evening?

3. Are you a morning person or an evening person? Why did you choose your answer?

4. What is the difference in time between your country and the country in which you are living now? When you came to this country, did the time change affect you in any way? How?

5. What is the difference between working a "night shift" and working a "day shift"? Which would you rather work? Why? In which shift would you expect your performance to be better?

PREVIEW

Directions: Read the title and any subheadings of the selection. Also look at the illustrations and read any captions. Then, without reading the selection, answer the following questions.

1. According to the title, what are affected by our "clocks"?

2. What do you think the author means by *clocks*?

3. Now, read the question and the answer given in paragraph 1. When do you think a 2,000-calorie meal is most fattening?

4. Read paragraphs 2 through 4. (This is one of the many studies

discussed in this article.) What do you think the purpose of the studies is?

5. Below are the parts of the experiments discussed in paragraphs 2 through 4. Fill in the blanks with the information described in these paragraphs.

conductor of experiment: ___Dr. Franz Halberg_____

subjects: _____

procedure: _____

result: _____

conclusion: _____

6. Glance at the first sentence of each paragraph in this selection. Which paragraphs discuss the following?

   I. Introduction: 1 through _____

   II. Relationship between time, drug administration, and treatment: _____ through _____

   III. Research in circadian rhythms: _____ through _____

   IV. *Zeitgebers* and dyschronism: _____ through _____
   Work shifts: _____ through _____
   Jet lag and the effects of travel: _____ through _____

   V. How diet affects our body's rhythms: 39 through _____

   VI. _____
   47 _____

   VII. Learning about your circadian rhythms: 48 through _____

   VIII. _____
   (conclusion): _____ through 57

READING

CLOCKS THAT MAKE US RUN

Our moods, health, mental acuity—all are under the sway of "Clocks that make us run."

LEN HILTS

1 Question: When is a 2,000-calorie meal fattening? Answer: That depends on what time you eat it.

2 Dr. Franz Halberg, professor of laboratory medicine and pathology at the University of Minnesota, probed this mystery in a study conducted a few years ago. Each day for a week, he fed six volunteers a single meal—eaten at breakfast time—that consisted of 2,000 calories. Then he gave the same participants the identical 2,000-calorie meal as *supper* for a week.

3 On the breakfast-only schedule, all six people lost weight. But on the supper regimen, four of the six *gained* weight. Even the remaining two lost more on the breakfast diet than on the supper diet.

4 Dr. Halberg's conclusion: A calorie is not the same at breakfast as it is at supper.

5 This study and hundreds like it at Harvard, Stanford, MIT, the University of California, and other institutions all point to the importance of timing. Investigations are increasing our understanding of the body's complex system of clocks and revealing that these rhythms can influence everything from mental health to worker productivity. In addition, these discoveries are spawning such new "rhythm" sciences as chronopharmacology, which examines the relationship between time and drug administration. Just as with food, the hour at which you take medication may be nearly as important as the medication itself.

6 For example, L-dopa, used in treating Parkinson's disease, disrupts the daily, or circadian, rhythms of lab animals when it's administered at certain hours. They suffer from what scientists call dyschronsim, symptoms of which include irritability, lack of concentration, and insomnia. When taken at another point in the animals' body cycles, the drug has no adverse effects. Such tranquilizers as Valium and some of the medications prescribed for hypertension may be influenced by chronobiological factors.

7 Furthermore, studies at the University of Arkansas and the University of Minnesota lend support to the theory that in some cases, circadian rhythms can influence the effectiveness of treatments.

8 In one trial, Lawrence E. Sheving, professor of anatomical sciences at the University of Arkansas, injected 300 mice with leukemic cells. He divided his "patients" into 12 groups of 25 and administered chemotherapy to all of them. Each group, however, received its medication at a different time. Sheving found that the cure rates differed: 52 percent of those receiving the chemotherapy at 5 A.M. were cured; only 16 percent of those receiving chemotherapy at 8 A.M. were restored to health.

9 Dr. William Hrushesky, assistant professor of laboratory medicine and pathology at the University of Minnesota, looked at this clockwork approach and applied it to a group of cancer patients. During the first phase of a two-part study, he alternated the times that two chemotherapy drugs were administered. Pat Quien, a patient with ovarian cancer, volunteered for the timed program. She noticed a considerable difference in her body's reaction to the drugs at certain hours. "You were back on your feet sooner if you took the cisplatin at six in the evening," she said. It appeared that there were certain hours of the day when a patient could better tolerate the drugs.

10 In the second part of this ongoing study, Dr. Hrushesky juggled three variables—the time, the order,

and the intervals at which the drugs were administered. His goal: to see whether "response and cure are also functions of *when* you get treated." The findings have been encouraging.

11   "We've had ten of the first twelve ovarian-cancer patients go into remission," he says. The results could be attributed "partly to the circadian time of treatment. It's likely to be an important part of why they're doing so well." Whether similar findings would be obtained on a large scale is yet to be learned.

ists at several research centers are also examining the relationship between circadian rhythms and depression. "Early data suggested—and it's still not proved—that some depressed patients have an internal circadian clock that may run too fast," says Dr. Daniel Kripke, professor of psychiatry at the University of California at San Diego. Approximately 40 patients have taken part in his studies to date. According to Kripke, lithium, which is an effective treatment for depression,

15   Although scientists have yet to understand all of the intricacies of circadian rhythms, they do know that each one of the body's hundreds of systems has its own timing. Body temperature and blood pressure rise and fall in the course of a day. Levels of hormones vary by as much as 80 percent. Heart rate is cyclical, as is iron concentration in the bloodstream. The white-blood-cell count may fluctuate by 50 percent during a day. And there is the sleep–wake cycle. Even your

---

Early data suggest that some of the patients who suffer from depression may have an internal circadian clock that simply runs too fast.

Hrushesky is currently seeking volunteers for his study—specifically, persons with ovarian or bladder cancer who've not been treated with chemotherapy.

12   In related studies, Dr. Erhard Haus, chief of pathology at St. Paul–Ramsey Medical Center, in Minnesota, discovered that some growths have their own temperature cycles, separate from the cycles of the surrounding healthy tissue. Other researchers have found that a spreading cancer is most vulnerable when it's growing and the cells are dividing fastest. It's conceivable, then, that matching the treatment to the time of the cancer's vulnerability could enhance the treatment's efficacy. Special-

slows down the body's rhythms. This occurrence lends credence to the clock/depression theory.

13   For the past 100 years, scientists have been publishing papers on the subject of circadian rhythms. At the turn of the century, educational psychologists conducted studies to see at what time of the day schoolchildren were most alert. Based on their findings, teachers designed schedules that slated difficult subjects, such as arithmetic, for the morning, when the children's performance was thought to be best.

14   Since then, interest in chronobiology has been cyclical, with knowledge in this area increasing rapidly within the past decade.

moods, activity level, memory, mathematical acuity, coordination, and sexual appetite have their own circadian patterns.

16   All of these systems operate independently. Yet they are marvelously synchronized in what may be one of the most intricate and complex mechanisms known to man. Control of the body's myriad systems is vested in a number of regulators, or clocks. Some of these are still unidentified; others have been recognized by their activity, but their locations haven't been pinpointed.

17   Scientists believe that they have located one of the key timekeepers in a tiny clump of cells in the hypothalamus, just above the point where the optic nerves cross as

they enter the brain. Called the suprachiasmatic nucleus (SCN), it cues sleeping, waking, and other activity patterns.

18   Researchers also suspect that a number of regulators lie elsewhere in the brain, in the adrenal glands, and probably in the liver. These control functions from hormone secretions to body temperature.

19   The links between this internal mechanism and the outside world are called *Zeitgebers* (German for *time givers*). These external factors cue the body's clocks and can even upset them. The earth's day/night cycle is a *Zeitgeber*. Stress can be one, and so can fear—as when the jet you are riding in plows through an area of extreme turbulence and turns you into a white-knuckled passenger. Social contacts, like stimulating conversations or painful verbal battles, can get the clocks ticking faster or slower. Food and drink are some potent *Zeitgebers*.

20   Our pacesetters will also react to a break in a daily pattern—traveling to a different time zone or changing your work hours, for example. In fact, chronobiologists cite shift work as a typical cause of dyschronism.

21   Changing shifts is not too different from flying from Tokyo to New York; in both cases, the internal clocks are set for one rhythm, but the body is moved to a place or condition that requires a different set of rhythms. As always, the clocks reset

themselves—and this usually happens within three to six days. But until then, the workers' body rhythms will be out of kilter.

22   The result can be more than worker discomfort. Scientists see an example of upset body clocks in the Three Mile Island nuclear-plant accident. The men at the controls changed shifts every week, on a rotational basis, which meant that their clocks were out of sync most of their time at work. As a result of this, chrono-biologists would expect them to have memory lapses and difficulty in focusing attention and in reacting quickly to a dangerous situation. The investigation of the accident bears this out. Throughout that night, up to 4 A.M. (when the accident started), there is evidence in the logbook of small errors in reading meters and interpreting data. "When shift workers have other than a normal daytime schedule or when they periodically change from one shift to another, their circadian rhythms become upset," explains Charles Ehret, a pioneer in the field of chronobiology and senior biologist at Argonne National Laboratory, in Argonne, Illinois. "This dyschronism is what the workers call shift-work fatigue. It isn't the good kind of fatigue that comes from skiing, tennis, or other physical activity. It is a condition of mental and physiological dysfunction, and it can impair job performance."

23   Impair it in what way?

Ehret says a worker might find a valve that is supposed to be closed—and open it. Workers suffering from dyschronism often do the opposite of what they intend to do.

24   Testifying in 1983 before the Committee on Science and Technology of the House of Representatives, Ehret noted that shift workers make up from 15 to 25 percent of our workforce in industrial cities. Those on such schedules include residents, nurses, and other hospital help; workers in many types of industry; firemen; policemen; air-traffic controllers; and pilots.

25   Restructuring work shifts to take timing into account would benefit both employer and employee, Ehret says. "These changes should result in improved production, prevention of catastrophes, prevention of minor injuries, and a reduction in absenteeism," he says. "On another level, they should reduce divorce, family conflict, and child abuse. We see loving and kind people made dyschronic; they develop gastritis and what appears to be a mean temper, and they do unacceptable things in the family circle. All these effects can be reduced."

26   Dr. Martin Moore-Ede, associate professor of physiology at the Harvard Medical School, helped to spearhead a work-shift study of employees at the Great Salt Lake Minerals and Chemicals Corporation, in

Ogden, Utah. Prior to the study, workers had rotated shifts weekly, always to earlier hours (from night to evening to day shifts). The result had been widespread insomnia and an increased potential for mishaps.

27   Moore-Ede recommended a schedule change to a phase-delay direction (to later hours, from day to evening to night). After this switch was made, company officials found that employees were more alert and more productive. "Shifts should rotate to later times with each rotation, and as much time as possible should be allowed between rotations," Moore-Ede told the same congressional science and technology committee. "If this pattern were followed, there would be less chance that a worker would have to perform a critical function when his alertness, reaction time, and body functions were at the low point of their daily cycle."

28   Other companies, such as Chicago's Commonwealth Edison, Houston's Exxon, and Canada's Ontario Hydro, are beginning to investigate their shift-work problems, and attendance is high at seminars given on the subject for business executives.

29   The same dyschronism that affects shift workers can also influence the performance of jet-setting businessmen. Again, winging your way across time zones can cause the various body rhythms to become displaced from one another, and sev-

eral days to three weeks may pass before systems synchronize once more. During the transition interval, you often feel terrible and function poorly.

30   How many critical treaties or business contracts have been negotiated after one of the negotiators has just stepped off an intercontinental jet? And how often has the negotiator failed to get the best terms simply because his clocks weren't working right? In 1956, John Foster Dulles, then secretary of state under President Eisenhower, flew to Egypt to conduct meetings on the Aswan Dam. Dulles withdrew an American offer to help Egypt build the dam, and later on, he attributed his poor judgment during the negotiations to jet lag. He had entered the meetings immediately after deplaning.

31   Aware of these dangers, military and government travelers, executives with companies like Control Data and Bechtel, and many other businessmen now adjust their travel schedules and diets before starting journeys that involve sensitive missions.

32   The effects of jet lag could also have an impact on sports teams that must travel appreciable distances to competitions. The U.S. Olympic Committee has underwritten a medical research project at the Harvard Medical School, to be completed this year, in the hope of documenting how circa-

dian rhythms affect athletes' performance.

33   "We are trying to understand such issues as the adaptation of athletes following the transition across time zones," says Dr. Charles Czeisler, who is the director of the project. "First, do these things matter to athletic performance? And if they do, what strategies can be developed to facilitate the adaptation of athletes who must travel long distances to events?"

34   An Olympic athlete, for example, may be in peak physical condition after months of training, but if his clocks aren't synchronized on the day of his event, he may not give a top performance. There is an even more distressing possibility: If his optimal performance hour is four in the afternoon and his event is scheduled for nine in the morning, he may lose a fraction of a second in time—just enough, in a world-class event, to prevent him from winning or setting a record.

35   Chronobiology research may provide part of the answer to another venerable sports question: What about the home-team advantage? Is it only a matter of having the crowd on your side and playing on familiar turf? Or do you also have an edge when competing against a team whose clocks are off a bit because the players traveled? Does this slightly affect their coordination— perhaps enough to cause a couple of dropped passes or

a few mixed-up signal calls? Circadian scientists suspect the latter to be true.

36 Is there a way to adjust the body's clocks so the effects of travel are diminished? Ehret tackled this problem and devised a diet regimen to minimize, if not prevent, the effects of jet lag. The diet employs certain cues —such *Zeitgebers* as rest, timed meals of high-protein or high-carbohydrate content, and coffee taken at specific times—that gradually reset the clocks, thus minimizing the malaise that many travelers experience after taking a lengthy jet flight. Caffeine manipulates the pacesetters, rescheduling certain natural cycles. Following Ehret's prescription, you can use this to your advantage when traveling. At other times, obviously, this resetting can cause problems.

37 "Some people never feel jet lag. Ehret explains that they "just do the right thing": They automatically—and unintentionally—set their clocks before and during a flight. They do this through their diet, sleep, work patterns, and coffee intake.

38 Not all scientists accept Ehret's findings. Timothy Monk, assistant professor of psychology in psychiatry at Cornell University Medical College, who is also engaged in jet-lag work, is currently testing some of the same components upon which the Ehret regimen is based. "Certain aspects of the diet plan are, I'm sure, very useful to travelers," he

remarks. "I don't believe, however, that the fasting and feasting alternation is of proved benefit at this time. The problem is that no control studies validate the Ehret study. The jury is still out." Even so, many thousands of people have used the diet when traveling, and most have found it effective. (Ehret's book, *Overcoming Jet Lag*, is published by Berkley.)

39 Ehret believes that as more is learned about the way food and drink affect our body rhythms, dietary concepts will be reexamined and will, in time, change. Oddly enough, it could be that in regard to timing and content, the farmer of 50 years ago knew more about eating than we do today.

40 He woke up, put away a protein-rich breakfast of steak and eggs, and then did a morning's work. At noon he ate dinner, his big meal of the day, which was also high in protein. He loafed a little after dinner before going back to work. At night, he ate a light meal, often high in carbohydrates.

41 This diet was absolutely right for his body clocks. When he got up in the morning, the systems had been set for go, the adrenaline was pumping, and he needed lots of fuel. The high-protein breakfast provided it. At noon, he had to replenish the fuel supply. Right after dinner, he rested. He recognized something scientists have since identified: the postprandial, or

after-meal, dip. The body's systems take a break after lunch. Most people blame this decline on having eaten lunch. Not so, unless you've really gorged yourself. It is simply a natural part of the body's cycling.

42 The farmer's light but carbohydrate-rich supper helped the body set itself on a glide path toward sleep. The carbohydrate meal stimulated the buildup of serotonin, which is the body's own sleep drug. Throughout the evening, then, the farmer continued on the glide path.

43 Compare the farmer's diet with one you may follow today. For breakfast, you eat cereal and sugar or perhaps toast and jelly, a carbohydrate meal that stimulates the serotonin and practically tells your body to go back to bed. And you pour in coffee, which further confuses your clocks by rescheduling the adrenaline cycle.

44 Lunch? Perhaps you eat a good one. Maybe you overdo the carbohydrates again. Then think of what happens when you sit down to a huge steak dinner, accompanied by coffee and stimulating conversation, at eight in the evening. The body has already begun its journey toward sleep. The serotonin level is building.

45 But the good conversation at the dinner table starts the adrenaline flowing. The protein stokes the system. The coffee and other stimulants reawaken the body and reset the clocks. By the time din-

ner is over, the body has been told to go *both* ways—up and down. You can anticipate trouble in getting a restful sleep, and also can expect the body clocks to be out of sync the next day. They may need the better part of the day to right themselves.

46   Further studies are required, of course, to support this theory on the importance of diet. "There is some evidence that food has effects, but thus far I think it's very preliminary," says University of California at San Diego's Kripke, who has been studying circadian rhythms for 20 years.

47   Circadian rhythms are not the same as biorhythms. Devised in 1887 by William Fleiss, these emotional and physical indicators are supposedly useful in predicting a person's good and bad days. The best that can be said about biorhythms is that it is a pseudoscience, like astrology, with no basis in empirical research.

48   You can get a fix on your own circadian rhythms by knowing your blood pressure, pulse rate, and body-temperature cycles, along with a few other test results, such as hand strength and eye-hand coordination. To determine your rhythms, take readings throughout the day and evening—perhaps a dozen in all. There's equipment available that provides excellent temperature, blood-pressure, and pulse ratings right at your own desk. Sporting-

goods stores sell a handgrip device with a meter on it.

49   After you have taken readings for several weeks, you'll detect a pattern. Highs, lows, and gradients in temperature, for example, will cover a 2°F span. You'll discover that the old idea of normal temperature being 98.6° is somewhat out of date.

50   The blood pressure readings may surprise you, too. Most of us think of blood pressure as a constant set of numbers. The fact is, blood pressure varies sharply each day. It's usually lowest in the morning, rises to a peak late in the afternoon, then goes down again during the evening.

51   The late Howard Levine, former director of medical education at New Britain General Hospital, in Connecticut, and a chronobiologist, liked to tell how careful he was about his blood pressure. For years he stopped at his physician's office in the morning and had his blood pressure taken. His doctor took a reading one afternoon, however, and the numbers were startlingly high. "Diagnosis of my condition, primary aldosteronism," Dr. Levine said, "was delayed a couple of years because I went to my doctor when my blood pressure was at its circadian lowest—and so it seemed normal."

52   The point is to take blood-pressure readings, and all other readings—every few hours. Log them and chart them for several weeks. Some of the readings may

be inconsistent. For example, if you take a reading while angry or upset, blood pressure and heart rate may be high. Eventually you will recognize any aberrant blips for what they are, and a true, usable chart will emerge.

53   The body-clock information you gather about yourself may help you to spot an illness in the making. An unusual pattern of readings from a system (temperature, for example) could indicate an oncoming illness, and you may wish to consult your doctor. Given this early warning, he may be able to diagnose and even treat the problem before it becomes full-blown.

54   Chronobiological research is extending into several other areas besides those touched on here. In addition to jet-lag and work-shift studies, investigators at the Institute of Chronobiology—part of the New York Hospital–Cornell Medical Center—are analyzing circadian rhythms' relationship to sleep disorders, depression, sexual and neuroendocrine problems, and aging. "There's some indication that sometime—and fairly rapidly—in the mid-fifties, there is a shift in the length of some of the internal rhythms," explains Daniel Wagner, assistant professor of neurology in psychiatry at the institute. "This may help us to understand why there's a tendency for people, as they get older, to go to bed earlier, get up earlier, and to nap." This reordering of the sleep cycle

and the need to rest during the day may not be just a consequence of more free time, Wagner points out. "It could show what happens to the rhythms due to aging."

55 The new findings in the field of chronobiology promise to improve our lives by providing us with some very powerful tools. Doctors will take body rhythms into account when prescribing drugs, timing them to the patient's circadian rhythms. Psychiatrists will have a new weapon against depression and other mental illnesses. Industrial-plant managers will plan shift changes so that their employees feel better, work more productively, and are safer.

56 Furthermore, we may see new world's records being set, as athletes plan travel and competition times to get the maximum effort from their bodies. Joggers will discover that keeping the body clock synchronized is as important as tuning up the muscles and the cardiovascular system. Calorie counters will begin to consider timing an important factor in diet regimens. And all of us can look forward to enjoying more days when we feel good and perform well because we have finally learned how to keep our body clocks ticking in synchronization.

57 Undoubtedly, we are on the threshold of the Circadian Age.

—Copyright 1984 by Len Hilts and reprinted with the permission of Omni Publications International Limited.

Postreading

TRUE OR FALSE

Directions: Decide if each of the following statements is true (T) or false (F) based on the selection.

_____ 1. The time a drug is taken plays a role in its effectiveness.

_____ 2. Although the experiments discussed in this article support theories, they do not prove these theories to be true.

_____ 3. A spreading cancer is most vulnerable when it is growing.

_____ 4. All body functions have their own circadian patterns.

_____ 5. The suprachiasmatic nucleus in the hypothalamus regulates all of the body's circadian rhythms.

_____ 6. Because workers at the Three Mile Island nuclear power plant suffered from dyschronism, they experienced memory lapses and had difficulty focusing attention and reacting quickly.

_____ 7. Rotating work shifts to earlier hours results in increased alertness and productivity in employees, while rotating shifts to later hours has the opposite effect.

_____ 8. According to Ehret, the effects of jet lag can be minimized by controlling various Zeitgebers.

_____ 9. If you know the patterns of your circadian rhythms, you will be able to predict whether you'll have a good day.

_____10. There is no "fixed" number that indicates a person's body rhythms.

_____11. Internal rhythms, Zeitgebers, body clocks, and biorhythms are all terms that have the same meaning as circadian rhythms.

_____12. Due to the work in chronobiology, scientists have been able to show a direct relationship between circadian rhythms and physical health.

READING WORKSHEET

Directions: After you have completed the true-or-false exercise, answer the following questions. You may refer to the selection if necessary.

216

1. Paragraph 1 consists entirely of a question and its answer. What purpose do you think this serves? _____

    _____

2. What purpose does the last sentence in paragraph 5 serve? _____

    _____

3. In paragraph 6, find the definition of *circadian*. _____

    _____

4. List the variables studied by Dr. Hrushesky (paragraph 10).

    a. _____

    b. _____

    c. _____

5. Choose the sentence that best describes the goal of Dr. Hrushesky's study.
    a. His objective was to determine when to give certain drugs.
    b. His objective was to determine if the time when a drug is given is a factor in how effective it is.
    c. His objective was to determine how many times to give certain drugs to see when they were effective.

6. Read paragraph 12. What is the clock/depression theory? _____

    _____

7. What is the suprachiasmatic nucleus (paragraph 17)? _____

    _____

8. What is a *Zeitgeber* (paragraph 19)? _____

    _____

9. What do you think the phrase *to be out of kilter* (paragraph 21) means? _____

    _____

10. The purpose of paragraph 21 is to
  a. introduce new information.
  b. summarize old information.
  c. define dyschronism.

11. After reading paragraphs 21 through 22, complete the following.

  Cause: _____

  _____

  Effects: Workers can experience memory lapse, difficulty focusing attention, and increased error in their performance.

12. List some of the symptoms of dyschronism suffered by shift workers.

  a. _____

  b. _____

  c. _____

13. What are some of the possible benefits Charles Ehret gives for restructuring work shifts? _____

  _____

14. What answer do you think the author expects to the question asked in paragraph 30? _____
  Why? _____

15. Locate the word *synchronized* in paragraph 34. Can you think of other words that begin with the prefix *syn-* (e.g., *synonym*)?

  _____

  What do you think this prefix means? _____

16. There are many questions asked in paragraph 35. Why do you think the author chooses to use questions instead of statements here?
  a. The author doesn't know the answers.
  b. People disagree about the answers.
  c. The questions have not been answered.

17. According to the article, what effect does a stimulant like caffeine have on the body clocks? _____

  _____

18. Choose the best paraphrase of the following sentence (paragraph 36): "Ehret tackled this problem and devised a diet regimen to minimize, if not prevent, the effects of jet lag."
   a. Ehret studied the problem and created a diet plan that might greatly reduce or even eliminate the possibility of problems resulting from jet lag.
   b. Ehret invented a diet plan that would reduce but not eliminate jet lag.
   c. Ehret worked on the problem of diet and created a plan that would minimally reduce but not prevent jet lag.

19. After reading paragraph 38, what inference can you make about Dr. Ehret's diet plan to help reduce the effects of jet lag? _____

_____

20. What do you think the phrase *The jury is still out* (paragraph 38) means? _____

_____

21. Find clues from the context to tell you the meaning of *late* in the first line of paragraph 51. (Hint: Look at the verb tenses used.)

What does *late* mean in this case? _____

22. What idea does the story involving Howard Levine illustrate?
   a. Blood pressure varies at different times of the day.
   b. There is a distinct pattern in a person's body temperature.
   c. You can improve your health by knowing your own body rhythms.

23. According to the author, what are some of the possible benefits from the findings of chronobiology?

_____

_____

24. You have probably noticed that the auxiliary *may* was used throughout this article. Look back and write down some of the verbs that it was used with.

   1. _____

2. _____

3. _____

4. _____

Why do you believe the word *may* was used so frequently? ____

_____

_____

INFERENCE AND RESTATEMENT

Directions: *Decide whether each of the following is a restatement (R), an inference (I), or a false statement (F) based on the selection. If the sentence is a restatement, locate the original in the selection and give the paragraph number where it is found.*

____ **1.** You will lose weight faster if you eat your largest meal in the morning.

____ **2.** There are differences between the chemical composition of calories eaten in the morning and calories eaten at night.

____ **3.** Treating cancerous cells when they are growing the fastest might improve the treatment's effectiveness.

____ **4.** Depression is caused by certain irregularities in circadian rhythms.

____ **5.** Charles Ehret has developed a diet that attempts to eliminate the effects of jet lag.

____ **6.** Even though Ehret's findings may lack evidence, his suggestions for minimizing jet lag have worked for many people.

____ **7.** Because Howard Levine never went to his doctor in the evening, he managed to postpone developing primary aldosteronism.

____ **8.** There are many aspects of chronobiology that have not been discussed in this article.

____ **9.** Circadian rhythms play a role in physical and psychological healthiness.

____ **10.** We should be able to extend the length of our lives as more and more research is completed in the field of chronobiology.

OUTLINING

Directions: Below is a partial outline of an excerpt from "Clocks that Make Us Run." Reread the selection and complete the outline.

Look at paragraphs 19 through 35. This section discusses two different types of dyschronism: (A) shift-work fatigue and (B) jet lag. Now begin outlining section A.

A. <u>Shift-work fatigue</u>

   1. Explanation

      a) Cause: _____

      b) Effect: _____

   2. Example: <u>Three Mile Island</u>

      a) Cause: _____

      b) Effect: _____

      c) Supporting evidence: _____

   3. Charles Ehret's work

      a) Definition of the problem: _____

         _____

      b) Answer to the problem: _____

         _____

      c) Results of changes:

         (1) Work aspects: _____

         (2) Social aspects: _____

         _____

      d) Experimental support

         (1) Conductor: <u>Dr. Martin Moore Ede</u>

         (2) Subjects: _____

         (3) Procedures: _____

         _____

         (4) Results: _____

         _____

Section B discusses jet lag. On another piece of paper outline the important aspects of this section. Try to set up your outline as was done for section A. Remember to organize your information in a fashion that enables you to refer to the important aspects quickly.

SKILLS CHECKUP: REFERENT RECOGNITION

Directions: *Check your understanding of referents by answering the following questions.*

1. In paragraph 5, what does *these rhythms* refer to? _____

2. Paragraph 14 begins with the phrase *Since then.* What does this refer to? _____

3. In paragraph 23, the word *it* appears twice. What two things are being referred to? _____

4. What are the *mishaps* the author is referring to in paragraph 26? ____

   _____

5. What are *these dangers* referred to in paragraph 31? _____

   _____

6. Who is *he* in paragraph 40? _____

7. In paragraph 47, what does *these emotional and physical indicators* refer to? _____

8. In paragraph 54, Daniel Wagner says, "This may help us." What does *this* refer to? _____

SUMMARY

Directions: *Write a summary of the selection. Include as many of the following words and phrases (or their related forms) as you wish. Begin with this sentence: Timing plays a very important role in how effectively our bodies do everything, from metabolizing food and accepting medication to adjusting to jet lag and shift work.*

travelers
circadian rhythms
dyschronism
athletes
Zeitgebers
chemotherapy

schedule
chronobiology
emotions
blood pressure
temperature

ESSAY QUESTIONS

Directions: In one to three paragraphs, answer the following questions using information from the reading to support your ideas.

1. What is dyschronism? Why does it occur? What are some of the effects of this phenomenon? Have you ever experienced dyschronism? If so, how were you affected?

2. Discuss how our lives might be improved by understanding our circadian rhythms.

3. What are biorhythms? Locate more information about biorhythms from magazine and journal articles and encyclopedia references. How do biorhythms differ from circadian rhythms? Why do you think the author wants to make the distinction between biorhythms and circadian rhythms clear?